Paulding Farnham

TIFFANY'S LOST

Genius

Saulding

Farnham

TIFFANY'S LOST Genius

by
John Loring

Harry N. Abrams, Inc., Publishers

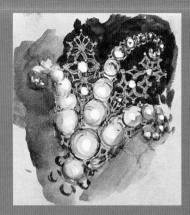

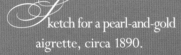

*S*ketch for a pearl-and-gold aigrette, circa 1890.

*P*reliminary sketch for Orientalist sapphire, diamond, and spun glass aigrette shown at the 1889 Exposition Universelle in Paris.

Previous pages 2–3:

*T*he swags of this elaborate necklace of diamonds set in platinum and gold were inspired by late-eighteenth-century French jewelry. Designed about 1900, it was made for Ellen Garretson Wade, wife of Jeptha Homer Wade II, a prominent Cleveland industrialist who collected gemstones with the advice of Tiffany's gemologist, George Frederick Kunz. The necklace can be divided into a bracelet and a shorter necklace, with or without the central swags.

Project Manager: Ruth A. Peltason

Editor: Sharon AvRutick

Designer: Carol Ann Robson

Library of Congress Cataloging-in-Publication Data

Loring, John.
    Paulding Farnham: Tiffany's Lost Genius / by John Loring.
        p. cm.
    ISBN 0–8190–3511–2
    1. Farnham, Paulding, 1859–1927—Criticism and interpretation.
    2. Jewelry—United States—Design—History. 3. Tiffany and
Company. I. Farnham, Paulding, 1859–1927. II. Title.

NK7398.F37 L67 2000
739.27'092—dc21   00–22807

Printed and bound in Japan

Harry N. Abrams, Inc.
100 Fifth Avenue
New York, N.Y. 10011
www.abramsbooks.com

Contents

The author and Tiffany & Co. would like to thank William R. Chaney, chairman of Tiffany's, and Michael Kowalski, president and chief executive officer of Tiffany's, for their confidence and support; Eric Erickson for his general dedication and enthusiasm, for his comprehension of Paulding Farnham's work and for his invaluable aid with the aesthetics of this book, and finally for his flair for finding seemingly unfindable images; Billy Cunningham and his associate Martin Friedman for so much of the book's splendid photographs; Kay Freeman and Rollins Maxwell for the thoroughness and relentlessness of their research, which has brought so much of Paulding Farnham's—and Tiffany's history—to light, as well as for their precision with captions, names, dates, and credits; Annamarie Sandecki, Tiffany's director of archives, for her help in exploring Tiffany & Co. archival materials; Louisa Bann, Tiffany's manager of research services, for her enthusiastic guidance through the many mysteries of Tiffany's monumental and much unexplored archives; Stephanie Carson, registrar of the archives, for orchestrating the photography of Paulding Farnham jewels and objects in Tiffany's collections; MaryAnn Aurora for her patience and wizardry at trafficking and coordinating all the complex materials and personalities that have gone into creating this book; Ruth Peltason, our editor, for her original vision and faith in this project and for her infectious enthusiasm for Paulding Farnham's work; Carol Ann Robson, our designer at Abrams, for the magnificent and imaginative layouts and graphics that bring out so clearly the unique qualities of Farnham's designs; Sharon AvRutick, our copy editor, for bringing grace to my somewhat cavalier use of language; Christie's and Sotheby's for the use of their remarkable photograph archives; Dr. Joseph and Ruth Sataloff for having preserved so much of Paulding Farnham's work at a time it passed unnoticed by others; Janet Zapata, once Tiffany's archivist in the 1980s, for her pioneer work on Paulding Farnham's history as well as for her pioneering articles in *Antiques* magazine on an assortment of his works; and last but far from least, Paulding Farnham's granddaughter Sheila Tinsley for her invaluable assistance with providing both Farnham family history and imagery for our book, a book which we sincerely hope will make all of his family as well as the entire world of design proud of her grandfather.

John Loring

Small flamboyantly colored pendant featuring Burmese rubies and green garnets.

aulding Farnham was catapulted to international celebrity at the age of twenty-nine, when to the astonishment of Old World designers, who thought they had a monopoly on such things, he won the gold medal at the Paris Exposition of 1889 for his Tiffany & Co. jewelry designs.

Success followed success, with Farnham's elevation to the position of head jewelry designer at Tiffany's in 1891 and an uninterrupted series of gold medals at those grandiose pageants of competition for mercantile supremacy, the Victorian era's great world's fairs: the Chicago World's Columbian Exposition of 1893, the Paris Exposition of 1900, and the Buffalo Pan-American Exposition of 1901.

Farnham's fortunes then abruptly changed. In 1902, Louis Comfort Tiffany—America's most celebrated decorative artist, with very different and, to give him his due, indisputably greater talents in design—inherited the control of Tiffany & Co. from his father, Charles Lewis Tiffany, the company's founder and Paulding Farnham's longtime patron.

The result was predictable. There was no room for two geniuses of the decorative arts in any house, even at Tiffany & Co., and Louis Comfort Tiffany was its largest shareholder.

The total eclipse of Farnham's career at Tiffany's was inevitable and rapid. When the St. Louis World's Fair opened in 1904, he was responsible for one jewel only, an extravagant Renaissance Revival necklace. His other works exhibited were a series of eclectic table furnishings in silver, gold, ivory, and gemstones. The Tiffany jewelry exhibit was the work of Louis Comfort Tiffany.

A drawing by Paulding Farnham in the Tiffany archives dated May 17, 1907 attests to the deterioration of the relationship between Louis Comfort Tiffany and Farnham. The drawing is for a "Tiffany souvinere [sic] spoon" and depicts Tiffany's world-famous Atlas holding, in place of a clock, a medallion of the then-new Neo-Renaissance Tiffany store at Thirty-seventh Street and Fifth Avenue topped by a symmetrical pair of Neo-Renaissance putti, so typical of Farnham's post-1900 designs. There is a slash mark through the putti and a notation in Farnham's handwriting, "Leave figures off. This change was ORDERED by Mr. L. C. Tiffany."

Some months later, Paulding Farnham left Tiffany & Co. His sketchbooks and press clippings, along with the photographs of his principal works, were relegated to a storeroom in a tower of the Tiffany silver factory in Belleville, New Jersey; and little was heard of his work again.

It is the mission of this book to publish a substantial portion of Paulding Farnham's long-lost designs now stored in Tiffany's archives and to restore his reputation to its rightful position. His preliminary drawings are vigorous and stylish as those of no other jewelry designer. His range was extraordinary, and his adroit use of Native American and Orientalist design vocabulary unique in the history of jewelry. He was a consummate colorist, and his floral jewels have no equal. He was, without contest, the greatest native-born jewelry designer our country has produced.

George Paulding Farnham—to state his full name—first came to the attention of the public on November 6, 1885, his twenty-sixth birthday, when the newsweekly *New York Town Topics* published an article on fashions in jewelry at Tiffany & Co., noting the rise in popularity of colored diamonds, semiprecious colored gemstones, and "reproductions of wild and field flowers in exquisitely enameled pieces."

The writer singled out one particular jewel: "A natural sized chrysanthemum made of purple and maroon-colored enameled gold is of the Japanese variety, having the thready, incurved petals. The disc of the flower is represented by a round, deep yellow diamond brilliantly cut. This is a brooch, and a design of Paul Farnham."

Family ties had brought Farnham to Tiffany's in his early twenties. His father, George Farnham, could claim an impressive American lineage, his ancestor Henry Farnham having come from Kenilworth, England, in 1644. The family of his mother, Julia E. Paulding Farnham, descended from Joost Pauldinck, a Dutch settler who arrived in the mid-1600s, and had been prominent in New York since shortly after the days the city had been the Dutch colony of New Amsterdam. Most significantly, however, Julia's older sister, Eleanor M. Paulding, was married to Charles Thomas Cook, vice president and later president of Tiffany & Co. and right-hand man to company founder and president Charles Lewis Tiffany.

Noting the artistic leanings of his nephew, Charles T. Cook had apprenticed him to study in the "Tiffany School," the studio of the company's chief designer, Edward C. Moore, where there was a strong primary emphasis on drawing and modeling from nature and secondarily a fascination with Orientalism. Both were not surprisingly combined in Farnham's first recorded jewel, the enameled-gold "natural sized" Japanese chrysanthemum brooch with its yellow diamond center.

Under the terms of Paulding Farnham's first contract with Tiffany's, on November 1, 1885, he graduated from being apprentice at the Tiffany School to serving as "general assistant" to Edward C. Moore in the design department, where he was paid the modest sum of fifty-five dollars a week. This was increased to sixty-five dollars a week a year later, and to a somewhat more lavish seventy-seven dollars a week the following November 1.

By early 1887, Tiffany & Co., like so many of the world's makers of luxury goods, was fully focused on preparations for the Exposition Universelle, the great world's fair that was to open in Paris in early May 1889 to celebrate the hundredth anniversary of the French Revolution.

The young Paulding Farnham in a photograph taken by Charles D. Fredricks & Co., 587 Broadway, New York, in about 1864. Tiffany & Co.'s store was then one block south, at 550 Broadway.

At home. Farnham's costume, hookah, fan, and furnishings bear witness to his fondness for Orientalism. The bearskin on the floor could well have served as a model for the "Bear and Bee" vinaigrette (scent bottle) he designed for the 1889 Paris Exposition.

Above:
Farnham's exhibitor's pass for the 1889 Exposition Universelle in Paris, where his jewelry won a gold medal and wide critical acclaim. He was twenty-nine years old at the time.

Left:
A 1901 photo of Paulding Farnham's wife— the former Sally James—and their St. Bernard, Sandy, at "Stepping Stone," their country house in Great Neck on the north shore of Long Island.

Sometime before his twenty-eighth birthday, Paulding Farnham, now regarded as Tiffany's young genius of jewelry design, was appointed by Moore to create the jewelry collection that Tiffany & Co. would send to the exposition. It would be two years in preparation and include roughly two hundred designs.

Tiffany's aim was to top its last successes in Paris, at the 1878 exposition, where its collections had won the grand prize gold medal for silverware for Edward C. Moore's "Japanesque" designs; the gold medal for jewelry; six medals for craftsmanship; and the star of a Chevalier of the French Legion of Honor for Charles Lewis Tiffany himself.

France had no less a goal for the 1889 exposition than to once and for all establish itself as the world leader in design, craftsmanship, and engineering.

It succeeded in the field of engineering with the show's centerpiece, Alexandre Gustave Eiffel's immense tower of iron girders, lattices, and trusses jutting a daunting 984 feet into the Paris sky and subjugating the imaginations of all who saw it. The exposition's Eiffel Tower of jewelry was Paulding Farnham's collection, particularly a small but magnificent collection of some two dozen enameled-and-jeweled gold orchids that were singled out by the press and public as the most original and outstanding jewels shown at the exposition. They earned Tiffany & Co. and Farnham a gold medal for jewelry.

Aided by Moore, who had developed a broad and rich palette of hard matte enamels for the colored patternings of his Orientalist "Sarasenic" silverwares and provided with dazzling collections of pearls and gemstones

With his children, James ("Jim") and Julia, probably photographed at "Stepping Stone" in the summer of 1901.

Tiffany's store, on the west side of New York's Union Square, where Farnham worked from the mid-1880s until 1905.

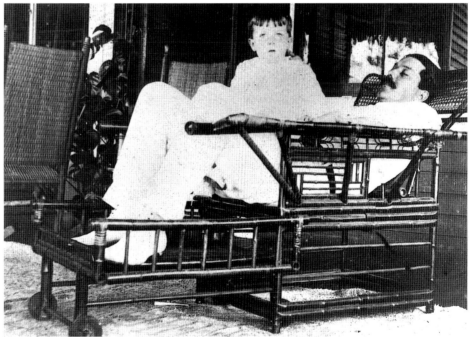

Sally and Paulding Farnham flanking two friends, one of whom holds their
son, Jim, at the beach in about 1900. That same year, the forty-year-old Farnham
won the grand-prize gold medal for jewelry as well as a gold medal for
silverware at the Paris Exposition.

Below:
Relaxing with Jim.

by George Frederick Kunz, Farnham created the greatest collection of jewels assembled by an American jeweler in the nineteenth century.

In a four-installment review devoted to the Tiffany exhibit, *The Jewelers' Weekly* called Farnham's work "a rare collection of costly and elegant ornaments and *objets de virtu*, unsurpassed in splendor by anything previously attempted" and concluded that "this wonderful collection excites the highest praise beyond the Atlantic and gratifies the national pride of visiting Americans." *The Jewelers' Circular and Horological Review* had already stated while the jewels were still on display at Tiffany's Union Square, New York, store during the second week of March 1889, "The whole exhibit is really the first attempt at a purely American art in jewel work, and the result is eminently successful, for the designs are not only original, but beautiful, while the workmanship is perfection itself."

The press knew no bounds in its praise of the young American designer and his jewelry for Tiffany & Co.

The Paris *Herald* of September 30, 1889, remarked that Tiffany's exposition jewelry was noteworthy for both its

> *boldness and originality of design. . . . Much of it is purely American, the designs and decorations being suggested by forms and ornamentation of basket and blanket work of the various tribes of North American Indians. All this jewelry has been designed and made under the eminently efficient and artistic direction of Mr. Paulding Farnham, the extent (if there really be any) of whose fertility of imagination and power of invention may be best judged by the fact that there are no two similar objects in the exhibit. This alone proves his artistic originality. . . . [T]he models themselves are due in many instances to direct studies from the Chillkat, Sitka, and Inuit Indians of Alaska, the Zuni and Navajo Indians from New Mexico, the Sioux Indians from Dakota, and the other Indian races of America.*

This dual focus of praise on Farnham's genius and on the pride America should take in his accomplishments was everywhere.

As the *Jewelers' Circular* summed it up, the man of the hour was "the chief designer, George P. Farnham, to whose genius the country is indebted."

The Paris Exposition Universelle of 1889 was, as desired, an even greater triumph for Tiffany & Co. than that of 1878. In addition to the gold medal for Farnham's jewelry, the firm received four other gold medals, one each for George Frederick Kunz's collections of precious stones of North America and North American pearls, one for leather goods, and one for engraving and printing. Edward C. Moore's Orientalist Saracenic and mixed-metal Japanesque silverware again won the grand prize for silverware, and Moore was made a Chevalier of the French Legion of Honor in recognition of his long-standing world leadership in silver design. There were also ten medals awarded to Tiffany craftsmen.

In *Marvels of the Exposition of 1889,* published in Paris, the author noted that American exhibits as highly evolved as Tiffany & Co.'s gave Europe pause. The author accurately explained that in America "the great fortunes that have burst forth in the last twenty years have created great needs in a taste for luxury and comfort" with the result that Tiffany's display cases boasted "magnificent examples of gold and silversmithing, a bit rich perhaps, but grand and sumptuous in their effect." Such were the tastes and demands of the Gilded Age, and Moore, Farnham, and Kunz knew the secrets of answering them.

Notwithstanding Tiffany's triumphs in jewelry, silverware, and other luxury goods at the exposition of 1889, and not entirely satisfied that the French had not somehow still bettered the competition in the international game of world's fair one-upmanship, less than a year after the exposition had opened, America signed the contracts setting in motion its answer to Paris 1889: the World's Columbian Exposition.

This great extravaganza of patriotic, mercantile, and architectural exhibitionism would celebrate the four-hundredth anniversary of Columbus' discovery of America and would be located in Chicago, the great metropolis of America's heartland.

The Chicago exposition was scheduled to open in May 1893, which made it clear that Paulding Farnham had little time to rest on the laurels of 1889. To add further pressure, shortly after Farnham's return from Paris, the health of his teacher and mentor Edward C. Moore deteriorated; and, although he was only in his early sixties, Moore died on August 2, 1891. Farnham was left not only to design the jewelry collections for the World's Columbian Exposition, but to oversee the silver collections as well. He, of course, would continue to be aided by the gemological genius of George Frederick Kunz; as well as by Moore's right hand in the silver department, John T. Curran, who would contribute his own remarkable designs for exhibition silver.

Edward C. Moore had been America's first major collector of Near Eastern Islamic Art. He willed the lion's share of his holdings (2,155 pieces in all) to New York's Metropolitan Museum of Art, where it remains to this day the foundation of the Near Eastern collections. For many years, Moore housed lesser but representative works in a small design museum located to the rear of the Fifteenth Street side of the main floor at Tiffany & Co.'s Union Square headquarters. Here, Farnham and the company's other designers and apprentices in the fourth-floor design department had access to the inspiration offered by an array of Near Eastern as well as Far Eastern design that reflected the breadth and refinement of Moore's taste.

Without Moore himself as a collaborator, Paulding Farnham would turn increasingly to his teacher's Islamic collections, which, by the early 1890s, were as yet unexploited in his jewelry design save for one extravagant "Indian" cat's-eye pendant made for the Paris 1889 Exposition. The influence of Edward C. Moore's love of Islamic art and Orientalist design would become apparent in Farnham's designs for Chicago and would later blossom in his collections for the Paris Exposition of 1900.

Although he abandoned neither his bent towards floral and animal motifs drawn directly from nature nor his fondness for the stylish and powerful abstract patterns of Native American design, Farnham would, however, fall in line with the universally revivalist themes of the World's Columbian Exposition and focus Tiffany's jewelry collection on Louis XV and Louis XVI Revival styles.

The Studio's December 14, 1889, review of "The House of Tiffany & Co. at the Paris Exhibition" had accurately forecast the unrivaled splendor of the jewelry display Farnham would design for the Chicago exposition, his first American world's fair: "With such a spirited and untiring lieutenant it may be safely predicted that if ever the present signs pointing to a World's Fair on this side of the water shall be fulfilled, the display that filled the Tiffany cases in Paris this summer will be far surpassed in taste and magnificence on that occasion."

The fair "on this side of the water" amply fulfilled *The Studio*'s prophecy. In Farnham's Tiffany display, there was magnificence beyond the public's wildest dreams, and there was informed taste in abundance. The Tiffany exhibits collectively won no less than fifty-six medals in Chicago.

There was, as in 1889, a remarkable variety of styles appropriate to the relentlessly eclectic and acquisitive bent of America's Gilded Age.

This was spelled out by American fashion's nineteenth-century bible, *Godey's Magazine*, in its August 1893 special report, "A Glimpse of the Tiffany Exhibit": "The general character of the jewelry exhibit made by the firm, reveals the most exhaustive study of all the earlier periods noted for their artistic productions; there are suggestions of the Giardinetto jewelry, the old Italian style of the fourteenth and the fifteenth centuries, old Hungarian, Russian, Turkish, Spanish, Egyptian, Portuguese, Grecian, Siamese, East Indian, Burmese, Javanese, Japanese, and the French of the Renaissance, the Empire, the Louis' and other periods."

Tiffany's photograph of its jewelry display at the 1900 Exposition Universelle in Paris, including Farnham's Montana sapphire iris brooch (lower left), "Aztec" necklace (top center), turquoise tiara (upper right), and "Wild Rose" corsage ornament (lower right).

Right:

iffany's 1900 photograph of an emerald-and-diamond tiara designed for the 1900 Paris Exposition.

TIFFANY & CO. EXHIBIT
PARIS EXPOSITION 1900
TIARA, EMERALDS AND DIAMONDS

Below:

ouis XVI Revival "Colonial" necklace of large yellow diamonds designed for the 1889 Paris Exposition. The lower pendant held the seventy-seven-carat "Tiffany II" Diamond, then the second largest diamond in America. It was cut in 1883–84 by Charles M. Field, inventor of the first modern diamond-cutting machine. Four years after the Paris Exposition, the Tiffany II Diamond reappeared at the World's Columbian Exposition, in the center of Farnham's "Canary Diamond Girdle" of woven Roman ocher gold set with twenty-one diamonds weighing a total of 450 carats. Its whereabouts today is unknown.

Below:

iffany's 1900 Paris Exposition photo of an elaborate necklace and pendant set with varicolored Montana sapphires.

TIFFANY & CO. EXHIBIT
PARIS EXPOSITION 1900

NECKLACE AND PENDANT
FANCY COLORED MONTANA SAPPHIRES

There was no doubt that Paulding Farnham's masterful works displayed in the Tiffany Pavilion at the northeast corner of the central court crossing of Columbia and Isabella Avenues in the massive Manufacturers and Liberal Arts Building was the most dazzling display of jewelry America had yet seen.

The Jewelers' Review summed it up: "The Tiffany diamonds would know no rival, and would lead all competitors."

Two showstopping parures—one of aquamarines and diamonds, the other of pink topaz and diamonds, and each including a necklace with a tiara and a generously oversized pendant—were central to Farnham's exhibit. Although the pink-topaz parure was listed in Tiffany's catalogue as medieval in style and the aquamarine set listed as "general style, conventional shells and sea weeds," both could more accurately have been folded into the World's Columbian Exposition's popular Louis XVI Revival.

Their innovation was in the lavish use of semiprecious gemstones accented with small diamonds to create important jewels at affordable prices, a radical departure from the ambitious prices of the "Colonial" and "American Hazelnut" diamond necklaces that Farnham had designed a few years earlier for the Paris 1889 Exposition. The timing was prescient, for the Gilded Age came to a jarring halt in 1893 when upheavals in the gold and silver markets sent America into a severe recession from which it would not fully recover until the turn of the century.

Following up on the Louis XVI Revival theme of Chicago, Farnham designed another splendid emerald, diamond, and pearl collar, this time in pure Louis XVI style, inspired by a necklace worn by a very young Marie-Antoinette in a portrait by François-Hubert Drouais in the South Kensington (now the Victoria & Albert) Museum in London.

Farnham also continued his designs of floral jewels, which had brought him so much attention with the orchids of 1889, with two much-remarked-upon large-scaled flowers in yellow sapphires: one a "Narcissus" corsage ornament with green-garnet leaves and ruby edging on the flower's petals; the other a "Spray of Moss Roses" hair ornament again with green-garnet leaves and stem.

Original to the Chicago display was a significant collection of Orientalist jewels. The centerpiece of this collection was a "Canary Diamond Girdle" fit for Scheherazade of colored woven gold set with twenty-one large canary diamonds weighing a whopping 450 carats. The central stone was the seventy-seven-carat "Tiffany II" Diamond plucked from the pendant of the "Colonial" necklace and still the second-largest diamond in America. (The "Tiffany" Diamond at 125.37 carats was the largest.) There was also a "Burmese" pendant of impressive proportion with a massive antique blue-green Russian aquamarine inlaid by Mughal craftsmen with gold and rubies from which garlands of Brazilian topaz and Burmese rubies cascaded down the bodice of the wearer. The intense and splendid color combination was revolutionary. The price was a mere one thousand dollars (around ten

*Farnham's aquamarine parure
is at the extreme left,
and his pink-topaz parure
is at the extreme right
in Tiffany's photograph
of its 1893 World's Columbian
Exposition jewelry.*

thousand in today's dollars). There was also an "Oriental Necklace, beryls in center of ruby and diamond ornaments"; a "Turkish Pendant, composed of a succession of diamond pendants arranged in Turkish fashion"; six Orientalist crescent brooches; an "Urchin Spray Aigrette" of antique Persian beads, a pear-shaped Peruvian emerald, diamonds, and pierced gold fit for a Persian prince; an "East Indian Armlet" of large emeralds surrounded by diamonds, tourmalines, yellow sapphires, and emeralds; and an "East Indian Bracelet" of nine chrysoberyls and small rubies.

Farnham's Orientalist jewels at the Columbian Exposition brought something fresh and unique to American jewelry design, both in their originality of form and, more importantly, in their audacious palette made up of the intensely colored semiprecious gemstones supplied by Tiffany's gemologist George Frederick Kunz.

Covered with glory from the abundance of prizes won by his designs at the World's Columbian Exposition and in total control of Tiffany & Co.'s design department, Paulding Farnham would continue his output of jewelry design, giving full play to his love of the exotic design vocabularies of both Oriental and Native American cultures acquired from Edward C. Moore as well as to his fascination with the rich and colorful world of gemstones spread before him in ever greater profusion by George Frederick Kunz.

Without Moore's leadership in Tiffany's silver department, Farnham also turned to silver design, drawing on his considerable talents as a sculptor. In 1893, at the time of the Chicago Exposition, Farnham was already at work on what would become one of the world's most celebrated nineteenth-century objects, the gold Adams Vase, presented to Edward Dean Adams in 1895 by the American Cotton Oil Company in gratitude for having "saved the company from financial ruin." In this most sumptuous of Tiffany presentation pieces, Farnham combined the opulence of his much-loved Renaissance Revival motifs along with more American references to the humble cotton plant. Over two hundred American semiprecious stones and pearls were encrusted in the elaborately detailed and intricately sculpted enameled gold surfaces of the nineteen-and-a-half-inch-high vase, which was eventually exhibited by Tiffany & Co. at the Paris Exposition Universelle of 1900. Four years later, it was given by Edward Dean Adams to the Metropolitan Museum of Art, where it remains on permanent display to this day.

The Adams Vase had scarcely been completed in Tiffany's workshop when Farnham began designs for America's most famous horse-racing trophy, the August Belmont Memorial Challenge Cup. Working from photographs of horses in August Belmont's racing stables, Farnham sculpted the legendary racehorses Matchem, Herod, and Eclipse for the design of three horses standing under a stylized oak tree surmounted by a finial of Belmont's father's favorite horse, Fenian. Although inspired by a classic 1835 William IV–style English trophy design by Paul Storr, the Belmont Cup is one of Farnham's rare adventures into the organic undulations of Art Nouveau, a style he undoubtedly felt better left to his employer's masterful and world-celebrated son, Louis Comfort Tiffany. The Belmont Cup was completed in 1896 and has not since been surpassed in horse-racing trophy design.

To celebrate the turn of the century, the French organized another grandiose world's fair, which in scale and attendance was to eclipse anything of its type before or since. At this blockbuster Exposition Universelle of 1900—which still holds the world's attendance record with some fifty million visitors—Paulding Farnham's Tiffany & Co. displays of jewels and silver once again won the gold medals. Farnham's design themes of nature's flora, Native American motifs, and Orientalism were those at which he most excelled and within whose boundaries he created his greatest works. They were central to his 1900 Tiffany displays.

With the exception of diamonds, the gemstones and pearls were almost all provided from American sources by George Frederick Kunz. The jewels themselves included some of Farnham's masterpieces such as the nine-inch-long Montana sapphire iris brooch (now in the Walters Art Gallery in Baltimore, Maryland); an equally large and splendid "Wild Rose" brooch, a magnificent "Aztec" necklace of Mexican fire opals; and a wealth of Orientalist pendants, brooches, and collars with exotic configurations and Farnham's highly original colorations. Demonstrating his continuing fondness for the strong

Completed in 1895, the Adams Vase was the centerpiece of Tiffany & Co.'s display at the 1900 Exposition Universelle in Paris, where a critic called it "a masterpiece of the goldsmith's art and a triumph for Mr. Farnham, the designer and modeller." In 1893, the directors of the American Cotton Oil Company commissioned Tiffany's to make the vase in honor of their chairman, Edward Dean Adams. They stipulated that it be "produced from materials exclusively American": thus, the yellow-green gold was mined in Forest City, California, the quartzes, spessartites, amethysts, tourmalines, and freshwater pearls all came from the United States, and the base is California gold quartz. The decorative motifs are based on Farnham's drawings of cotton blossoms and branches. The male figure on this side of the vase represents Genius, and the partly nude female figure on the opposite side is Modesty. Farnham wrote, "The two youthful figures on the foot represent the young Atlas turning the financial world at his pleasure, his hand resting on the ornamental beaver to convey the idea that he is sensitive to the presence and importance of industry. The opposite figure represents the new country and Husbandry, holding a cotton-branch in his hand." Mr. Adams presented the vase to New York's Metropolitan Museum of Art in 1904.

and stylish abstractions of Native American design, Farnham's Tiffany silver exhibit featured a "Navajo" vase and "Hupa" and "Zuni" bowls with metallic-black niello patterns and encrustations of New Mexico and Arizona turquoise and freshwater American pearls.

Following the Paris Exposition Universelle of 1900, the United States would celebrate the arrival of the twentieth century with the Pan-American Exposition, held in Buffalo, New York, in 1901.

With the Pan-American Exposition following fast on the heels of Paris 1900, Paulding Farnham would be pressed for ideas to satisfy the press and public's thirst for the new. The two collections would have to overlap, and whatever returned from Paris could, of course, be shown in Buffalo; however, a new theme would have to be introduced. Inspired by the high praise heaped upon his Renaissance Revival triumph, the Adams Vase, at the 1900 Paris Exposition, Farnham turned for inspiration to the far-from-American late French Renaissance, or so-called Henry II, style and created a collection of Renaissance Revival jewels populated by superbly sculpted miniature gold wood nymphs as well as by witty and slightly more American squirrels and rabbits.

His skill in mixing colored gemstones and colored pearls was masterful in these pieces.

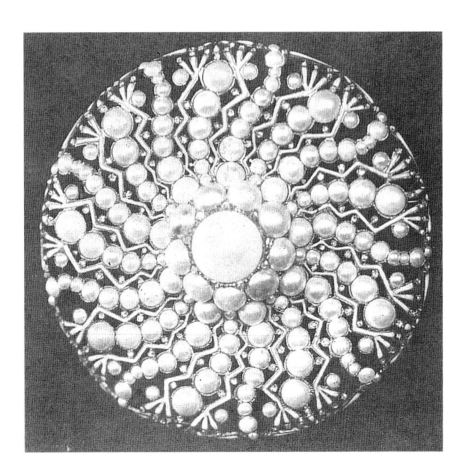

With Farnham's established commitment to end-of-the-nineteenth-century free-wheeling eclecticism, his collections for Buffalo embraced styles as diverse as Viking, Pompeian, Louis XV, New Zealand, Byzantine, and East Indian. To the latter style belonged an astonishing "Pendant in the East Indian style," to quote from Tiffany's catalogue: "diamonds

Opposite:

The August Belmont Memorial Cup was made in 1896 for the winners of the Belmont Stakes; it was commissioned by August ("Augie") Belmont II in honor of his father, the prominent banker and sportsman who founded the Belmont Stakes in 1867. The trophy's oak-leaf decoration and acorn form symbolize the origins of thoroughbred bloodlines ("great oaks from little acorns grow"): the horses represented on the base of the cup, Eclipse, Herod, and Matchem, were bred in England in the eighteenth century, and every thoroughbred is descended from one of these three sires. Augie Belmont's horses Hastings, Henry of Navarre, and Merry Prince stood as models for Farnham's sculptures. The horse forming the handle of the lid represents the senior August Belmont's Fenian, who won the Belmont Stakes in 1869. When Hastings won the Belmont Stakes on June 2, 1896, Augie Belmont ordered two cases of wine opened to christen the Tiffany cup that he had commissioned.

Left:

The "Hupa" brooch shown at the 1889 Paris Exposition. Tiffany's listed it as "*Brooch. Shaped after the decoration of basket work of the Hupa Indians, California.*" On June 6, 1889, *The Jewelers' Weekly* reported, "A brooch of Miami Valley pearls, set in an enameled gold mounting in imitation of the basket work of the Alaska Indians, is a strictly American jewel. It contains 175 pearls, that in the centre being a very large one. There is a neat setting of diamonds about the center pearl and along the curved arms of the design. The brooch is valued at $650."

TIFFANY & CO. EXHIBIT
PAN-AMERICAN EXPOSITION
BUFFALO 1901

NEG. NO. 2417

Tiffany's 1901 photographs of three jewels designed for the 1901 Buffalo Exposition.

Above:
This imposing corsage ornament had an enamel and diamond-pavé "Napoleonic" laurel wreath studded with varicolored pearls, a large rose-cut diamond in the center, and a diamond ribbon terminating in pear-shaped pearls.

Left:
The center of this East Indian-style pendant is a 64.56-carat cat's-eye flanked by stylized palm fronds set with white and yellow diamonds; suspended below are a 28.31-carat ruby surrounded by diamonds and a 101.25-grain mauve pearl. It was priced at $16,000.

Opposite, above:
Tiffany's photo caption for this pendant reads, "Large emerald pendant, three large emeralds suspended by a delicately woven ribbon with leaf work to carry out the ornament."

fashioned into the shape of palm leaves, in the center of which are pear-shape yellow brilliants. Also yellow brilliants forming the top ornament. All this suspending a large cat's eye (of 64.56 carats) in the center; and suspending a large ruby (of 28.32 carats) with a fancy diamond setting, to which is suspended a large (101 grain) mauve pearl."

More arresting than all this, however, was a life-size pink carnation corsage ornament to rival the Montana sapphire iris of the previous year, and a collection of Farnham's most abstract jeweled floral sprays of great beauty, boldness, and purity of design.

The Jeweler's Circular of June 29, 1901, waxed euphoric about the nature themes of Paulding Farnham's newest collection: "In the Paris Exposition, American jewelry won many deserved laurels, and some of the displays at the Buffalo Exposition show strikingly the marvelous development of this art in our country. The Tiffany exhibit is a blaze of splendor, and the gems, gold and silver objects, enamels, etc., are veritable works of art."

TIFFANY & CO EXHIBIT
PAN-AMERICAN EXPOSITION
BUFFALO 1901

NEG. NO. 2402

Below:

After the New York preview of Tiffany's exhibit at the 1900 Paris Exposition, the *New York Times* reported on March 17, 1900, "One of the most exquisite pieces of jewelry was a wild rose branch set in iron, toned to the proper color scheme. Pink tourmalines were used together with pear-shaped emerald drops and marquise-shaped emeralds in the leaves, with diamonds and topazes to complete the flowers." Set with ninety-one pink tourmalines, twenty-seven emeralds, one yellow topaz, and 164 diamonds, the "Wild Rose Branch" brooch was priced at a whopping $24,000.

TIFFANY & CO. EXHIBIT
PAN AMERICAN EXPOSITION
BUFFALO 1901

NEG. NO. 2412

WILD ROSE BRANCH PINK TOURMALINE
EMERALDS AND DIAMONDS

TIFFANY & CO. EXHIBIT
PARIS EXPOSITION 1900

Left:

Tiffany's 1901 photograph of the "Lawson Pink" carnation corsage ornament shown at the 1901 Pan-American Exposition in Buffalo. The flower contained 28 tiny diamonds and 240 pink tourmalines totaling over 119 carats; the calyx, stem, and leaves were pavéd with 176 green garnets. The corsage ornament was priced at $3,000.

Farnham would have little time, however, to bask in the glory of grand-prize gold medals awarded to his jewelry and silver collections.

On October 6, 1901, his patron and employer, eighty-nine-year-old Charles Lewis Tiffany, fell and fractured his hip, and on February 18, 1902, three days after his ninetieth birthday, he died.

Artistic control of Tiffany's fell into the hands of his son Louis Comfort Tiffany, now head of the family, who gave himself the new title of design director of Tiffany & Co.

Paulding Farnham had collaborated with Louis Comfort Tiffany at times, designing gold-and-jewel mountings for some of his Art Nouveau iridescent "Favrile" glass vases and perfume flasks for the Paris Exposition of 1900, but it was obvious that the new design director had no sympathy for his father's head designer nor for his vision of American design which, for all its much recognized excellence, remained adamantly rooted in the nineteenth century and its revivalist tendencies.

Tiffany Studios glass would take the place of honor in Tiffany's display at the Turin International Exposition of Modern Decorative Arts in 1902. There were no Paulding Farnham jewels shown. In fact, the only Farnham pieces that were included were his Viking-style coffee service and vases from Buffalo along with his Burmese-style dressing-table set, which had already been shown in both Paris and Buffalo.

Two years later, Tiffany & Co.'s display at the Louisiana Purchase Exposition held in St. Louis in 1904—the last of the series of great international trade expositions that had begun with London's Crystal Palace of 1851—would center on an extensive collection of Louis Comfort Tiffany's naturalistically enameled and painterly jewels. Based on humble native American plants and flowers such as Queen Anne's lace and dandelions, these jewels had little in the way of gemstone ornamentation.

Paulding Farnham would be allowed to contribute only one jewel— a massive Renaissance Revival enameled-gold-and-diamond necklace— to the exhibit of the company whose image as the undisputed world leader in jewelry design he had done more than anyone else to create.

Tiffany's 1904 photograph shows part of the elaborate, almost monumental, Renaissance Revival silver tea and coffee service designed for the St. Louis Exposition in 1904. Note the winged figures on the handles.

Farnham's clay maquette for the gilt
sculpture of Psyche,
the White Rock sparkling water
trademark, for the company's exhibit
at the 1904 St. Louis Exposition. The
sculpture stood in a miniature neoclassic
pavilion with a stained-glass dome
designed by Louis Comfort Tiffany.
Farnham also used winged female figures
on the Renaissance Revival silver service
he designed for the exposition.

Below:
Farnham sculpted the dog Nipper
for Tiffany's life-size version
of the world-famous "His Master's Voice"
trademark shown by the Victor Talking
Machine Co. at the 1904 Louisiana
Purchase Exposition.

Other examples of his work were displayed: a vast and intricate
Renaissance Revival silver tea and coffee service, along with an intricately
crafted series of jewel-like Renaissance Revival objets d'art including
a gold dressing-table set and a gold Burmese-style inkstand topped with
the carved and inlaid tip of an elephant tusk and a "Giardinetto"-style
timepiece decorated with figures of the wood nymph Pomona and the
goddess of love and poetry, Erato. Farnham's love of Native American art
was evidenced only by one rather humble gold watch with whale and bear
motifs inspired respectively by the far Northwest's Queen Charlotte
Island Indians and the Testline tribe. All were highly praised by the art
magazine *International Studio*; however, the last of Farnham's great
Native American–style objects—his remarkable "Aztec" bowl of sterling silver and copper set with semiprecious stones—which would have
brought him far greater honor as a creative artist, was only completed
by Tiffany's silver and jewelry shops on August 31, 1905, too late to
bring him credit at the St. Louis World's Fair.

Farnham stayed on at Tiffany & Co. under the authority of Louis
Comfort Tiffany, as long as the new design director's power was moder-
ated by the presence of Farnham's uncle Charles Thomas Cook, who
had become Tiffany & Co.'s president on the senior Tiffany's demise.
Cook himself, however, died at seventy-one on January 26, 1907.

On June 2, 1908, at only forty-eight years of age, Paulding Farnham
left Tiffany & Co.—and jewelry and silver—for good. He would devote
the remaining eighteen years of his life to painting and sculpture. In the
twenty-two and one-half years he spent with Tiffany & Co., Farnham's
work won more honors both at home and abroad than any other jewelry
designer of his time and brought Tiffany & Co. and the United States
international respect as the undisputed leader in jewelry design during
the last decade of the nineteenth century.

Nature

During the period from the late 1860s to the early 1880s, when Edward C. Moore was building both Tiffany's design department and his own studio, known as the Tiffany School—where Paulding Farnham was to receive his design education—art in America had a single dominant theme: nature.

Since the 1840s, America's cultural identity had been rooted in nature and in the country's quasi-religious admiration of the sublime, the beautiful, and the picturesque as perceived in its geology, flora, and fauna.

No one in New York was more knowledgeable about art and design than Edward C. Moore; and his Tiffany School, in line with the sense of the times, functioned on the Tiffany credo "Mother Nature is the best designer." Not only was the Tiffany design library filled with illustrated botanical books, but the design department contained a vast collection of dried and pressed botanical specimens. The apprentice-students spent a considerable part of their time producing drawings and watercolors of plants and flowers.

John T. Curran, Paulding Farnham's contemporary in the Tiffany School, would use his training in botanic illustration to produce the greatest triumph of American metalwork, the Magnolia Vase, shown at the 1893 World's Columbian Exposition; and Paulding Farnham would use his to produce some of the greatest jewels ever made in America, among them, enameled floriform brooches and hair ornaments for the Paris Exposition of 1889 and jeweled floral corsage ornaments for the Paris Exposition of 1900 and the Buffalo Pan-American Exposition of 1901.

While his early floral jewels in the last half of the 1880s were so realistic as to be almost botanically accurate in their form and color (if not in their addition of diamonds and colored gemstones), they were direct latter-day expressions of the aesthetics of New York's Hudson River School landscape painters Thomas Cole, Frederic Edwin Church, Thomas Moran, Albert Bierstadt, and, of course, the popular painter of orchids Martin Johnson Heade. Their art-world universe revolved about New York's Tenth Street Studios, which were only a few blocks from Tiffany & Co. and with which all the Tiffany designers were well familiar.

By the 1890s, however, the Hudson River School had been displaced by the more modern American Impressionism of such artists as Childe Hassam, William Merritt Chase, and Winslow Homer, and the realist visions of America as the second Eden and of the wonders of untouched nature as symbols of hope and purity—as well as of opportunity—were crumbling.

Perhaps for this reason, Farnham produced only a very few floral jewels for the 1893 Chicago World's Columbian Exposition, outside of some

Renaissance Revival "Giardinetto" pieces. Inspired by fifteenth-century Italian design, these jewels had no connection to the Hudson River School's vision of America as the second paradise.

Farnham's nature-inspired jewelry for the Chicago World's Fair focused not on the beautiful aspects of nature's flora but on the picturesque aspects of her fauna. He produced an abundance of jeweled amphibian, reptile, and insect life: frogs, snakes, dragonflies, caterpillars, butterflies, and beetles.

Amongst all this miniature jeweled menagerie, one truly remarkable jeweled spray of "Moss Roses" featured carved yellow-sapphire buds and green-garnet–pavé leaves reflecting the time's more impressionistic view of the beauty of nature.

Farnham would pursue this new direction with the magnificent "Iris" and "Wild Rose" for Paris and with the "Lawson Pink" carnation and a series of almost abstract floral brooches for Buffalo's World's Fair of 1901.

He would create additional floral pieces for the next few years; by the time of the St. Louis Louisiana Purchase Exposition of 1904, he had abandoned floriform jewelry altogether.

Enamel, gold, and diamond rose brooch designed about 1890. There was a great demand for enameled floral jewelry following the success of Farnham's orchid jewels at the Paris Exposition of 1889.

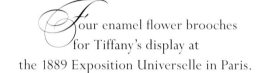

Four enamel flower brooches
for Tiffany's display at
the 1889 Exposition Universelle in Paris.

Above left:
A heliotrope—*Heliotropium arborensis (voltarieanum)*—
brooch, with diamonds in its florets and in the
veins of its bright green leaves.

Above, right:
A gentian-like brooch with diamond anthers
and gold leaves.

Left, center:
A floral brooch (possibly a Korean lilac) with
diamond-pavé leaves.

Left, bottom:
A mignonette—*Reseda odorata*—brooch. The Paris
Herald commented, "It is simply marvelous, the
stamens being only the thinness of a hair, yet having
two colours in enamel, while even the smallest part of
the flower is reproduced." Tiffany's made this version
of the brooch in 1890: the 1889 version
had diamond-pavé leaves.

Opposite:
Circa 1899 drawing for a hydrangea brooch. The
completed hydrangea brooch was set with sapphires
from the banks of the Missouri River near Helena,
Montana; prospectors looking for gold discovered
sapphires at this site in 1865.

The popularity of lilac brooches in the late nineteenth century was partly due to the Empress Eugénie's purchase of a large all-diamond lilac brooch designed by Léon Rouvenat that was displayed at the 1867 Paris Exposition Universelle. Farnham's lilac brooch, designed circa 1888, is quite similar in form, if not in treatment, to Rouvenat's. The florets are enamel with diamond centers, and the leaves are gold.

Flower brooch drawings.

Top:
Circa 1888 sketch of a lilac bloom for an enamel, diamond, and gold lilac brooch.

Bottom:
Wild tulip brooch, circa 1904.

 Drawing for a plum brooch—half frosted
rock crystal and half frosted amethyst—shown
at the 1900 Paris Exposition.

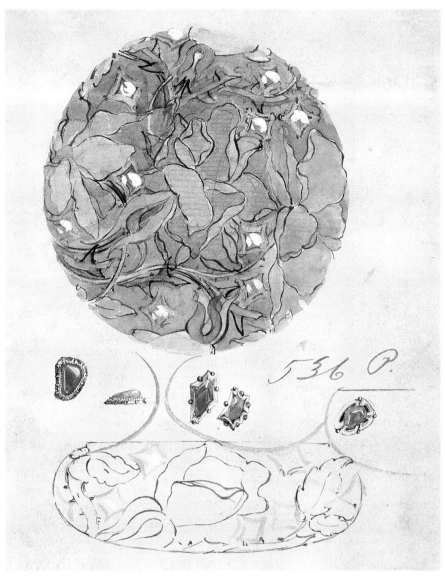

$\mathcal{D}$rawing for a gold-and-enamel bonbonnière studded with Tennessee pearls and depicting a climbing rose, shown at the 1889 Paris Exposition. Bonbonnières were small jeweled candy boxes that nineteenth-century ladies often wore suspended from belts with fancy chains. (The cabochon azurites below the drawing were probably intended for another bonbonnière.)

$\mathcal{T}$he gold and pink-enamel "American wild rose" lady's lapel watch with diamond-pavé leaves and stem was made for Tiffany's display at the 1889 Paris Exposition. *The Jewelers' Weekly* commented, "This is an elegant piece of workmanship and justly commands marked attention. Its price is $600."

Below:
Preliminary sketch for the watch.

he final drawing for the green-garnet
hair ornament shown at the
Chicago Exposition. Tiffany's May 1893
catalogue listed it as the "Raphael Head
Ornament" with "diamond in cluster with
feathers of demantoids"; it was priced at
a modest $900.

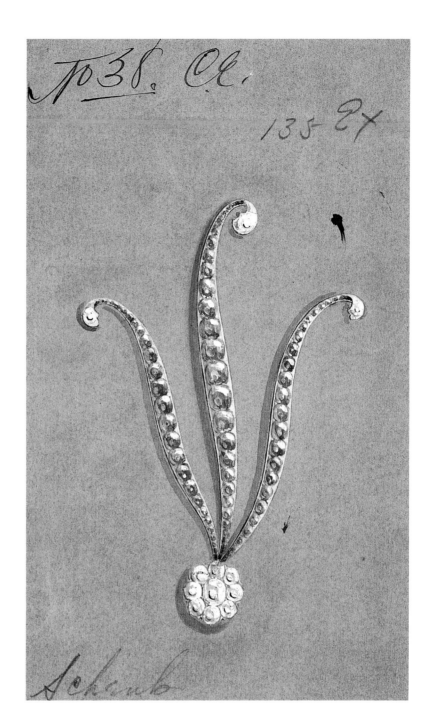

 reen-garnet brooch in the form of
a willow leaf, designed about 1893.
Farnham and Tiffany gemologist
George Frederick Kunz were especially
fond of green demantoid garnets
from Polderwaja in Russia's
Ural Mountains.

The spectacular iris brooch set with Montana sapphires, green garnets, and diamonds was shown by Tiffany & Co. at the 1900 Paris Exposition. In *The Art Interchange,* one critic enthused, "The fine gradations of velvety iridescent color, the beautiful curve of the petals and the delicate joints in the long stem, as well as the marked originality of the design, afford the lover of really fine metal work pure delight." He added, "The American visitor at the Paris Exposition will look with pride and satisfaction upon the display by Tiffany & Co. and this feeling will be enhanced when they learn that the products are notably American, both in the materials employed and the workmanship which enters into their fashioning. In the matter of design they are produced wholly from original and novel ideas emanating from the alert American mind of Mr. Paulding Farnham, the art director of the house, who has for the past two or three years been planning this display and under whose energetic and tireless supervision has been worked out the marvelous collection of artistic goldsmith's work a collection that would find few rivals in the aggregation brought together in the great fair." Railroad magnate and art collector Henry Walters purchased the brooch at the exposition, and it is now at the museum he founded, the Walters Art Gallery in Baltimore.

Opposite:

Foreground: pink-tourmaline and green-garnet iris brooch that Paulding Farnham presented to his wife, Sally James Farnham, who had admired the Walters iris brooch at the Paris Exhibition. Background: Tiffany's 1900 photo of the Montana sapphire iris brooch.

TIFFANY & CO. EXHIBIT
PARIS EXPOSITION 1900
IRIS BROOCH SAPPHIRES

70

NEG. NO. 1903

FULL SIZE

35

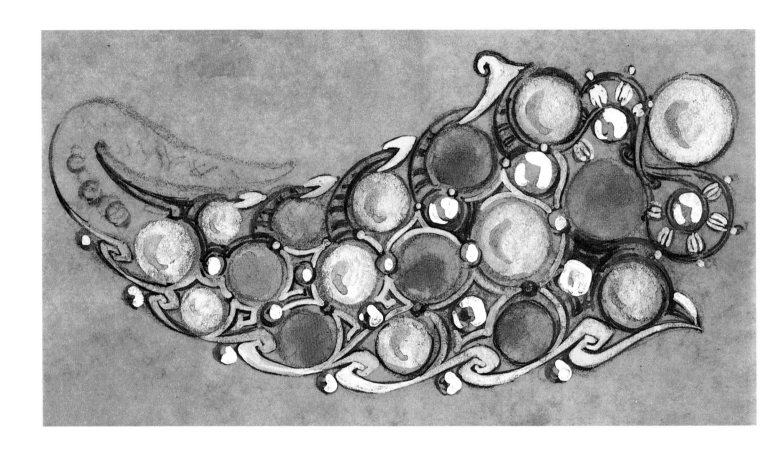

 rawings for the "Florida Palm" enamel brooch made for the 1889 Paris Exposition. The final brooch was set with ten pink pearls from the Miami River in Ohio, five moderate-sized diamonds, and a Montana sapphire. *The Jewelers' Weekly* called it "very handsome" and "elegant."

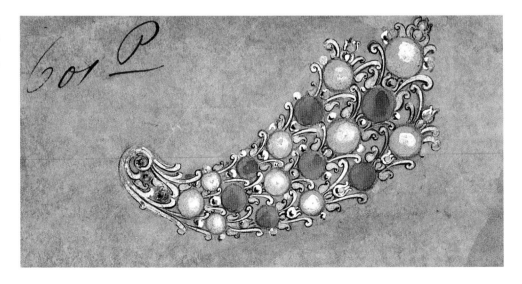

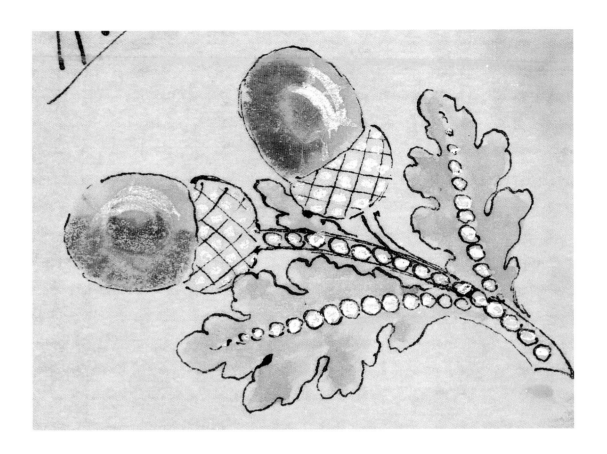

Drawings for an acorn brooch with diamond-studded leaves
and stems, circa 1895. Farnham would produce the quintessential
acorn design with his Belmont Cup of 1896.

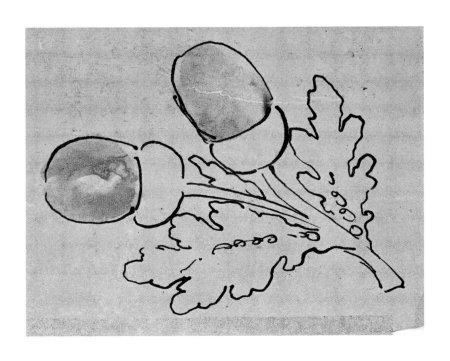

The spectacular chrysanthemum brooch of Unio "dog tooth" pearls from the Mississippi Valley is the mate to a brooch made in 1904 for the jewelry-collecting musical comedy star Lillian Russell, often referred to as "Diamond Lil."

Daisy brooch set with baroque pearls and diamonds of the same period.

Above and opposite:
These diamond floral branch brooches designed in 1901 for the Buffalo Pan-American
Exposition were far more abstract than Farnham's previous floral designs.

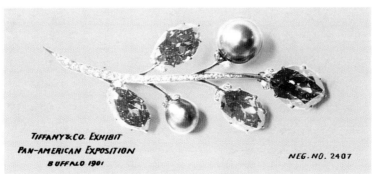

The designer himself hand-colored the 1901 photo.

Design for a Queen Anne's lace brooch, which Louis Comfort Tiffany may have adapted for his Queen Anne's lace hair ornament shown at the 1904 St. Louis Exposition. Gustave Stickley, the guiding force of America's Arts and Crafts movement, wrote in *The Craftsman* that Louis Comfort Tiffany's hair ornament was "realistically treated and shown at the height of its bloom. In the center of each section of the flower, fine opals are massed for the production of color-play, and each petal is worked out individually in minute detail; while the center of the entire blossom is set with garnets and diamonds, which emphasize the sectional divisions, and serve to increase the fire of the opals."

"Ivy" necklace of diamonds set in gold-backed silver, designed circa 1900.
The necklace originally came with a frame so that it could be worn as a tiara.

Opposite:

Pearl-and-diamond spider brooches made for the 1889 Paris Exposition.

Above:

A circa 1889–93 "Napoleonic" bee pin with ruby eyes, diamond-pavé wings, rose-cut diamond thorax, and pear-shaped pearl abdomen. The pin is placed upon Farnham's original drawing.

"Beetle" brooch of emeralds and diamonds set in green gold designed for the 1893 World's Columbian Exposition in Chicago, where Farnham's other insect brooches included a sapphire beetle, two diamond butterflies, and a cabochon emerald fly.

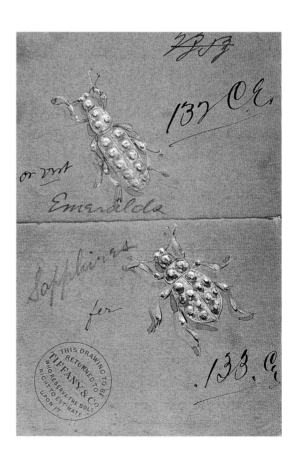

Original drawing for the "Beetle" brooch.

The "Bees and Honeysuckle" vinaigrette shown at the 1893 Chicago Exposition. The bottle, made of agate from Yellowstone National Park, is carved with a honeycomb pattern; the honeysuckle flowers are silver, and the gold bees have yellow-sapphire wings and red-garnet eyes. Both the bottle and ornament are studded with green garnets. (The prominent yellow sapphire in the original top has been replaced with an amethyst.)

Below:
Farnham's sketch.

irca 1893 rock-crystal scent bottles ornamented with gold animals
encrusted with green garnets, diamonds, and rubies. Left: a lizard stalking
flies; right: a rattlesnake with a seed-pearl rattle confronting a bird.

Orchids

No floral jewelry has ever attracted as much attention from the press, the jewelry industry, and the public as the two dozen enameled orchid brooches and hair ornaments that Paulding Farnham designed for the Paris Exposition Universelle of 1889.

Exotic orchids began to be shown in North America around the time of Tiffany's founding in 1837, and the first spectacular specimen to be seen by Americans at home and to inspire New York botanists and collectors with its opulent beauty was a *Cattleya mossiae* imported by the prominent florist Isaac Buchanan in September 1840. Some ten years later, there were American collections of hundreds of species of the exotic flowers, and a first manual for orchid growers was published in 1852.

Orchids became a symbol of wealth and prestige during the two decades of the Gilded Age (circa 1873–93) and were cultivated in the greenhouses of many of the rich and socially prominent of New York and Boston.

The Hudson River School painter Martin Johnson Heade furthered the craze with his popular, colorful, and romantic series of paintings of South American orchids and hummingbirds that he began around 1870 and continued until his death in 1904.

By the time of the 1889 Paris Exposition, the Gilded Age's fascination with orchids was at its peak; and by the time that fifteen of Farnham's orchid jewels were displayed from March 10 to March 16, 1889, at Tiffany's Union Square, New York, store before being shipped to the Paris Exposition, their audience had long since succumbed to orchid fever.

The *New York Tribune* of March 15, 1889, reported: "The most unique and interesting feature of the exhibit is seen in the brooches. Here are gold enamelled orchids of fifteen varieties each as perfect in its way as the product of nature. The stems are made green with emeralds. The coloring of the leaves is marvellous beyond description, testifying to the extraordinary skill of the designer as well as to the artistic sense and exquisite taste of the enameller. Nothing more beautiful can be imagined than the general effect of each plant."

On April 7, 1889, the *Syracuse Herald* added: "Jay Gould, who is a great orchid lover, and whose orchid houses up in Irvington-on-the Hudson contain the finest private collection in the world, was particularly enthusiastic over these imperishable reproductions of his favorites, and was a heavy purchaser, not meaning them for female wear, but to be kept in a cabinet for his own personal delectation."

The orchids met with equal enthusiasm in Paris. The Paris *Herald* of September 30, 1889, noted that Mr. Paulding Farnham's

> *greatest triumph is to be found in the "orchid" exhibition, the most popular corner of Messrs. Tiffany's show. This corner consists of a series of twenty-four species of orchids, which are so faithfully reproduced that one would almost doubt that they are enamel, so well do they simulate the real flowers. Among these are the Vanda, Coerulea, Saccolabium Giganteum, Phalaenopsis Schillerianum; Coelogyne Cristata, Dendrobium Nobile from East India; Odontoglossum Maculatum, Odontoglossum Inseley Leopardinem, Oncidium Tigrinum, Odontoglossum Cervantesii, Oncidium Varicosum Rogersii, Oncidium Orinthorynchum from Mexico; Odontoglossum Landreanum, Odontoglossum Alexandrae, Odontoglossum Harryanum...; Cattleya Bicolor, Odontoglossum Zygopetalum, Laelia Harpophylla from Brazil; Calanthea Veitchii Hybrid from Veitch's Nursery, London; Chysis Liminghi from Guatemala; Angraecum, Eburneum, Incidium Konesianum from Paraguay.*
>
> *These are embellished in part with diamonds of white and brown, and other colors, the stems being made of diamonds, emeralds, pearls, and in one instance a row of minute rubies—a ruby being set between each emerald and stem in such a manner that at a distance it has the appearance of fuzz or hair.*
>
> *The jeweler's skill in copying nature's forms and colourings by the process of modelling and enamelling gold, is shown not only in the imitations of orchids, which are simply marvellous, but in the pieces of jewellery, which, though almost absolute copies of nature, are not merely artificial flowers, but by peculiar treatment and the introduction of precious stones form unique and highly artistic articles of jewellery.*

The general enthusiasm for Farnham's orchid jewelry was such that the following year, in April 1890, Tiffany's extended its offerings from twenty-four to thirty-nine varieties.

Passion for the orchids has not diminished over the years. On October 20, 1993, one of the 1890 series of enameled orchids sold at Sotheby's New York for $415,000.

Farnham designed a series of twenty-four jeweled enamel brooches, each depicting a different variety of orchid, for the Tiffany's exhibit at the 1889 Exposition Universelle in Paris. Their brilliant success led to the production of further versions of the original brooches, along with a new series of brooches depicting other orchid varieties, which were first shown at Tiffany's New York store in April 1890. According to the *New York Herald*, "The Easter exhibit of orchids at Tiffany & Co. is larger, more varied and more beautiful even than their exhibit at the Paris Exposition." Left: Orchid Brooch N° 45, depicting an *Oncidium jonesianum* from Paraguay, was made in 1890. The stem and the border of the labellum (lip) are diamond pavé. Right: the flower for Orchid Brooch N°18 is similar to a *Vandopsis parishii* from Burma and Thailand, but Farnham labeled his drawing "Chyisi Liminghi," a species that is native to Guatemala. (Such mislabeling of exotic orchids was common at the time.) The prominent column is diamond pavé, and the stem is diamond-and-ruby pavé. This brooch was shown at the 1889 Paris Exposition. Tiffany's listed the 1890 version as "Concolor Tonkinese," and the *Herald* reported that "it looks so fragile that it seems the slightest breath would wilt its delicate beauty."

Opposite:

This 1890 version of Orchid Brooch N° 19 has a diamond labellum and a bright-red, yellow, and brown column. It sold at Sotheby's New York in 1993.

Above right: Orchid Brooch N° 49 was made in 1890. Farnham labeled his drawing "Laelia Eyermanii," but it may have been a *Laelia gouldiana*, a Mexican variety named for the orchid-collecting tycoon Jay Gould, who purchased several of Farnham's orchid brooches at the 1889 Paris Exposition. Center: made in 1890, Orchid Brooch N° 44 depicts a *Cattleya schilleriana* native to Brazil's Espírito Santo mountains, which are famed for the fine aquamarines mined there. The large patterned column is studded with diamonds, and the stem is diamond pavé. Bottom left: this version of Orchid Brooch N° 19 was shown at the 1889 Paris Exposition. Bottom center: Orchid Brooch N° 14 depicts an *Oncidium tigrinum* native to Mexico; this version was made in 1890. It has a diamond in its labellum and a ruby stem. Bottom right: a *Dendrobium nobile,* native to the cool foothills of the Himalayas, was the subject of Orchid Brooch N° 70, made in 1890.

Farnham's flower drawing for
Orchid Brooch N° 19,
illustrated on pages 52 and 53. He labeled it,
"Phalaenopsis Schillerianum East India," but it was probably
an *Odontoglossum* from Luzon in the Philippines.

Right:
rawing of a *Dendrobium nobile* native
to the cool foothills of the Himalayas for
Orchid Brooch Nº 70.

Below:
rawing of a Colombian *Odontoglossum crispum*
for Orchid Brooch Nº 67.

Right:
arnham's drawing for Orchid Brooch Nº 17,
an *Angraecum eburneum*
from Madagascar.

*O*rchid Brooch N° 4 depicts a *Calanthe veitchii*, a cross of *Calanthe vestita* by *Calanthe rosea* (both tropical Asian orchids) from Veitch's nursery in London.

No 2 = 555 P Saccolabium Gigantum East Ind...

2

No 148+

No 151+

Within the drawing: 54 · Orchid #49 / Pearls or dias · (Page 209) · Vanda Sanderiana · Laelia Eyermanii

Within the left drawing: No 155+ · No · No 154 · No 149+

Above:

Drawing of an *Evanthe sanderiana,* native to Mindanao in the Philippines, for Orchid Brooch Nº 54. Right: drawing for Orchid Brooch Nº 49. Farnham labeled the drawing "Laelia Eyermanii," but it may have been a *Laelia gouldiana* native to Mexico. Brooches based on these two drawings were made in 1890.

Left:

Orchid Brooch Nº 2 represents a *Saccolabium gigantium* from the Philippines, a compound flower of many florets on a single stem. Farnham enlarged a single floret for the brooch. Foreground: a version of Orchid Brooch Nº 2 made in 1890 (the Paris 1889 version had a diamond-pavé stem); its column is topped with a diamond. Background left: the original sketch of the floret. Background right: Farnham's drawing for five orchid stickpins includes a version of Orchid Brooch Nº 2 at extreme left.

Above:

Orchid Brooch N° 8 depicts an *Odontoglossum maculatum*, which grows in Central America. The column is topped with a diamond, and the three tan-brown petals are bright—not matte—enamel, unusual for the series. This version was made in 1890; the one shown at the 1889 Paris Exposition had more irregular petals, a diamond-pavé border on its labellum, and a diamond-pavé stem.

Opposite:

Orchid Brooch N° 17a is an *Odontoglossum constrictum* native to Venezuela and Colombia. Farnham labeled his drawing "Sandreanum Columbia." This appears to be the version shown in Paris in 1889, missing two of its six original florets.

Native American
DESIGN

During the first half of the nineteenth century, the notion of America as largely an unspoiled wilderness inhabited by an indigenous population of picturesquely ornamented savages, who were (as all savages in the Romantic vision) "noble," occupied a favored place in the American collective consciousness.

The nation's vast unexplored territories beckoned as a symbol of purity, hope, and, naturally, opportunity for territorial and economic expansion.

The artist George Catlin was the first to promote the West and its colorful inhabitants, through paintings he completed on an 1832–34 expedition up the Missouri River and westward. His work, which was exhibited on the East Coast and in Europe around the time of Tiffany's founding, eventually inspired Tiffany silver design in the early 1890s.

By the time of the 1845 publication of Tiffany's first catalogue, the Native American arts and crafts and design vocabularies were becoming familiar on both sides of the Atlantic. Tiffany's promoted "INDIAN GOODS: Moccasins, Dresses, Pipes, Belts, Pouches and the various fancy articles, made of Birch Bark, embroidered with Moose Hair, all of which are suitable for presents to friends on the other side of the water."

Walking in Catlin's footsteps, other artists soon began to promote the West as well. Thomas Cole's close friend Henry Cheever Pratt accompanied and documented in hundreds of sketches and watercolors U.S. Boundary Commissioner John Russell Bartlett's United States–Mexico boundary survey in 1850–53. Other Hudson River School artists would soon follow, first in search of exotic or "sublime" wilderness material to satisfy their wealthy East Coast clients; and, after the opening of the transcontinental railroad in 1869, in support of the railroad barons and the burgeoning tourist industry.

The great icons of "Hudson River School" Western painting were produced in this period. Frederic Edwin Church painted his definitive image of Mexico, *Cotopaxi*, in 1862. Albert Bierstadt painted *Valley of the Yosemite* in 1864. Thomas Moran added *Grand Canyon of Yellowstone* in 1872 and *Chasm of the Colorado* in 1873–74.

By the time of Paulding Farnham's arrival at Tiffany's design department around 1880, the firm had not only long been selling Native American arts and crafts but had also made a number of important pieces of exhibition silver featuring detailed sculptures of Native Americans. Most notable were two massive thirty-five-inch-high, five-hundred-ounce candelabra made around 1875 for James Gordon Bennett, Jr., the publisher of the *New York Herald* and one of the Gilded Age's most spectacular profligates. The imagery of these monumental pieces, shown at the 1878 Paris Exposition, included exultant Indian warriors brandishing both scalping knives and scalps, along with more peaceful Indian braves paddling birchbark canoes. The candelabra were accented with bison heads, war shields, tomahawks, spears, and feather headdresses.

Another extravagant and publicized piece of Tiffany silver featuring Native Americans was the "Comanche" trophy commissioned in 1876 by the father of American horseracing, August Belmont. It showed a spear-wielding Comanche warrior in full battle-attack position shielded by his galloping horse. This and other Native American–inspired Tiffany trophies were the work of a talented, if academic, French-born silversmith and sculptor, Eugene J. Soligny, working under Edward C. Moore's direction.

Paulding Farnham shifted the direction of Tiffany's Native American designs from Soligny's fanciful depictions to far more original designs that employed a bold and stylish vocabulary of Native American symbols, pictograms, and decorative devices applied to forms derived from Native American pottery and basketwork.

The first important body of this work by Farnham was exhibited at the Paris Exhibition of 1889 and received considerable and favorable attention from the press. In April 1890, *The Jewelers' Circular and Horological Review* enthused:

> The striking feature in the collection…leaving aside its magnitude, value and beauty, resides in its being of thoroughly American character. Not only did the artisans whose hands wrought these beautiful objects receive their training in the Tiffany shops, but the designs of the principal part of the collection are of pure American character, being a refinement to the point of perfection of the graceful and quaint forms which have been unearthed among the rude implements made by the native American Indians. The chief designer, George P. Farnham, to whose genius the country is indebted for the collection is as much American as it is possible to be.

Amidst the revivalist styles of the World's Columbian Exposition of 1893, Farnham produced only two Native American jewels: a Wisconsin pearl, diamond, and enameled-gold "Navajo Indian" brooch, and a ruby, American pearl, enameled-gold, and diamond "American Indian" brooch.

But for the Paris Exposition of 1900, he designed the most spectacular of his Native American jewels, the "Aztec" necklace whose glowing orange fire opals recalled the "lurid fire" of the sky, as Church himself described the sunset in *Cotopaxi*.

Paulding Farnham also employed his Native American style outside his jewelry collections, and some of the most original and remarkable pieces of American metalwork ever produced are his "Pueblo" bowl inlaid with both copper and niello for Chicago 1893 and his "Zuni," "Hupa," and "Navajo" bowls for Paris 1900. His final important work of Native American design, the "Aztec" bowl, was completed at Tiffany's in 1905, unfortunately too late to be included in the Tiffany display at the 1904 Louisiana Purchase Exposition in St. Louis.

Two of the three pieces of Native American–inspired silver designed for the 1900 Paris Exposition. A critic writing in *The Art Interchange* in May 1900 thought Farnham's Native American–inspired designs surpassed one of his most celebrated pieces: "In silver articles nothing more original either in shape or in treatment could be found than the bowls, hammered out by hand from single pieces of silver, following the shapes of Zuni and Hupa Indian baskets.... To the artist's eye they seem better worth the thought and care bestowed upon them than the more elaborate Adams Vase."

Above:
Silver, inlaid niello, and turquoise bowl based on Zuni baskets.

Opposite:
Silver and Arizona turquoise vase based on Navajo pottery: the "corncob" handles contain a total of 322 American freshwater pearls.

Right:
Copper and niello inlaid silver cup and saucer with a Navajo blanket pattern circa 1890.

Opposite, above:
The third Native American–inspired silver piece designed for the 1900 Paris Exposition. Tiffany's catalogue described it: "Silver and copper. Hammered up by hand, of one piece. Shape taken from a Hupa Indian basket. Style of silver inlaying represents a flight of wild birds. The handles are conventional rattle-snakes, set with American turquoise."

Below:
Silver-and-copper "Aztec" bowl mounted with semi-precious stones, completed by Tiffany & Co. on August 31, 1905.

Farnham designed four silver "Pueblo" bowls for Tiffany & Co.'s display at the 1893 Chicago Exposition, basing their shapes and patterns on pottery made by the Pueblo tribes of New Mexico and Arizona.

Below:

This Pueblo bowl is unusual in several respects: it is studded with twelve faceted rubies; it bears the inscription "Souvenir of America from Nellie"; and its patterns are inlaid yellow, green, and pink enamel rather than copper and niello.

Right:

N° 27 in Tiffany's Chicago Exposition catalogue, this Pueblo bowl has four repoussé clusters of regional plants labeled greasewood, sagebrush, sacred thorn, and mesquite.

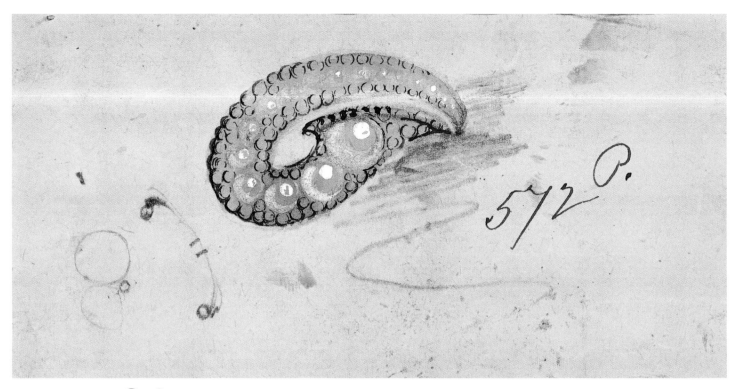

A sketch for a Native American–inspired pearl brooch designed for the 1889 Paris Exposition.

The "Sioux Indian Shield" brooch made for the 1889 Paris Exposition. Tiffany's listed it as "*Brooch.* Shape from the decorated horse-hide shields used in warfare by the Sioux Indians, Dakota, pearls from the Cumberland River, Tenn., and emeralds."

Right:
Preliminary sketch with a pentagonal design.

Below:
Tiffany's 1889 photo of the finished hexagonal brooch.

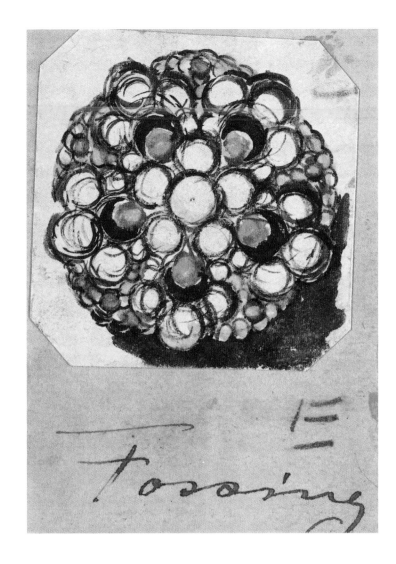

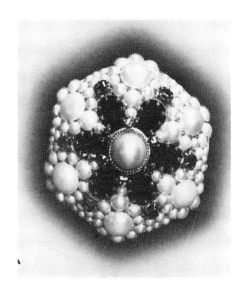

A group of Native American–inspired jewelry designs for Tiffany & Co.'s display at the 1889 Paris Exposition. Left center: the catalogue description for this item read: "*Brooch.* Decoration, 'Bur Marigold,' wild flower of the Southern United States. Pearls from Tennessee." Center: the ring made to this design was described as "Pink pearl from the Miami River, Ohio, and brilliants from Brazil, South America." Right center: this ring was described as having "Decoration and shape taken from the Navaho Indians, New Mexico. Sapphire." Above right: the brooch made from this drawing was listed as "*Brooch.* Decoration, study from the Sitka Indians (Esquimaux), Alaska. Tourmaline." Farnham marked the drawing "Thompsonite," referring to a stone found on the shores of Lake Superior, but a tourmaline from Auburn, Maine, was used in the brooch instead.

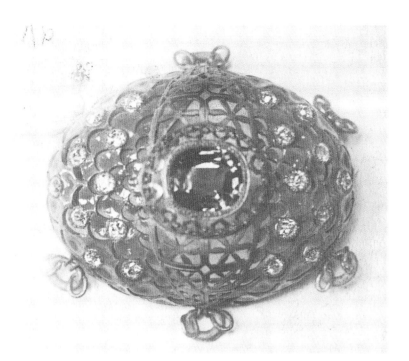

Two Farnham designs for Native
American–inspired brooches
shown at the 1889 Paris Exposition.

Left:
"Sitka" brooch. The central tourmaline came
from Auburn, Maine; the golden beryls, from
New Milford, Connecticut.

Above:
Basketwork brooch with "essonite yellow" spessartite garnets from Amelia, Virginia,
and red garnets (also called "Arizona rubies") from Fort Defiance, Arizona.
The Jewelers' Weekly noted, "A spessartite garnet brooch is a very handsome jewel.
Two large garnets are set as the centres of peculiarly formed flowers, and a third,
still larger, is set in a square pendant, suspended to the brooch by one of its corners.
The design is derived from the work of the Chilcat Indians. The stones are very fine and
are elegantly shown in their tasteful mountings." There was considerable confusion about
the name of the tribe: Tiffany's photo caption called it "Huper" (i.e., Hupa),
its catalogue, "Navahoes," and *The Jewelers' Weekly*, "Chilcat."

The "Aztec" collar, designed for the 1900 Exposition Universelle in Paris and shown again the following year at the Pan-American Exposition in Buffalo. The Princess of Wales (later Queen Alexandra) made diamond and pearl collars fashionable when she began wearing them to conceal a scar on her neck. Farnham advanced the fashion by using vividly colored stones—forty-five Mexican fire opals and sixty-four red tourmalines—set in thick Roman gold, and he added a ball-shaped pendant set with twenty-six pink and red tourmalines. The *New York Times* reported on March 17, 1900, that the collar was "said to form the finest collection of Mexican opals in the world." Tiffany's priced the jewel at $3,500.

Farnham's original drawing of the "Aztec" collar shows it with a pendant, as does Tiffany's photo of 1900. The pendant was subsequently removed.

TIFFANY & CO. EXHIBIT
PARIS EXPOSITION 1900
COLLAR-FIRE OPALS

Farnham designed several Native American–inspired match safes for the 1889 Paris Exposition.

Left:
A gold match safe with green enamel ornamentation based on Navajo basketwork with a cabochon California gold quartz on its top.

Below:
A drawing for another match safe inspired by Native American design, this one topped with a desert mouse.

Opposite:
Drawing for five Native American–inspired match safes.

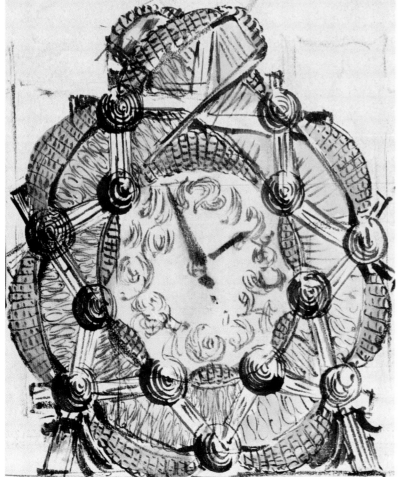

Above:

Two preliminary studies for a card case studded with cabochon sapphires shown by Tiffany's at the 1889 Paris Exposition; the design was based on Native American embroidery.

Left:

A clock design based on a Native American war shield.

Opposite:

One of a pair of Mexican fire opal bracelets designed to accompany the "Aztec" necklace. Gypsy Rose Lee's second husband, William Alexander Kirkland, gave her the bracelets on her fortieth birthday, January 9, 1954. The greatest burlesque queen of all time, Gypsy Rose Lee also collected nineteenth-century paintings, furniture, and jewelry.

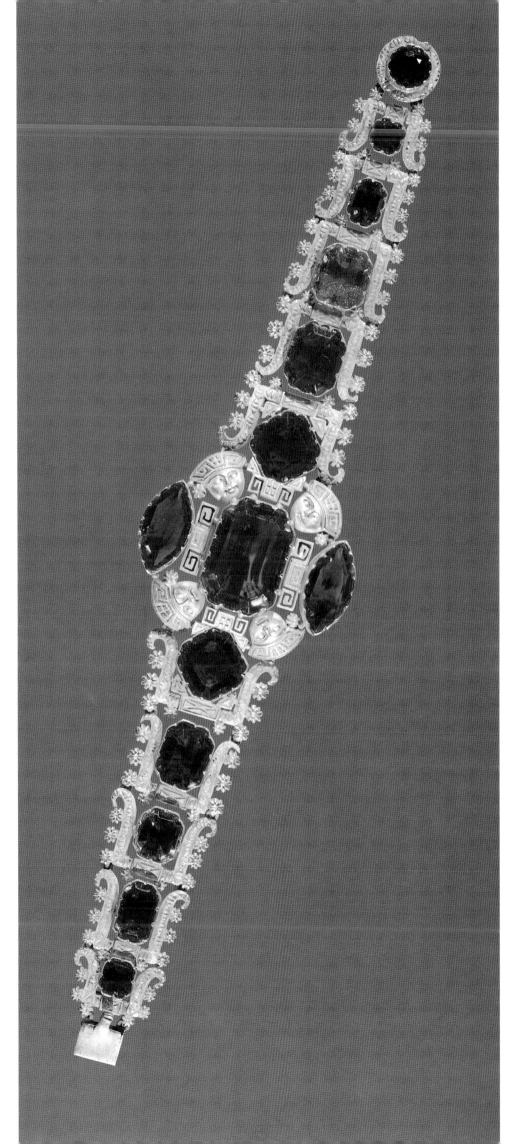

Orientalism

In the second quarter of the nineteenth century, Orientalism, or the West's reinterpretation of the arts of Islam (and, to a degree, the arts of Hindu India) began to take root in the American consciousness. Following the interruption of the Civil War, the style grew to almost universal popularity among the country's monied classes until the more modernist tastes of the first years of the 1900s came to dominate.

Tiffany & Co. played its own significant role in Orientalism's progress. From the beginning, the firm recognized the style's importance; and, in fact, used an Islamic cartouche to frame its logo for the letterhead of its second store when it opened at 271 Broadway in 1841.

Tiffany founder Charles Lewis Tiffany, like all educated Americans, would have read Washington Irving's bestseller *The Alhambra*, published in 1832, which set so many of his countrymen to dreaming of Islamic castles in Spain. Some years later, in 1846–48, his friend and fellow entrepreneur P. T. Barnum would further focus Tiffany's awareness of the style when he built his early Orientalist mansion, Iranistan, in Bridgeport, Connecticut. In 1874, Tiffany's head designer Edward C. Moore, the greatest American collector of Islamic art of his time, began producing Islamic-style silver for Tiffany; and, in 1876, the Philadelphia Centennial Exposition, where Tiffany & Co. had award-winning exhibits that included Moore's Islamic-style silver, boasted no less than six Moorish-style entertainment pavilions. These brought a taste for Orientalism to a far greater audience, and with it a far broader market for Orientalist design.

By 1878, two years after the Philadelphia exposition, Charles Tiffany, by then a confirmed believer in Orientalism's commercial merits, brought the first significant jewels in that style to America when he purchased three important Orientalist diamond necklaces from the deposed Queen Isabella II of Spain and resold them to San Francisco's queen of diamonds, Mrs. Leland Stanford.

In the early 1880s, when Paulding Farnham was studying in Edward C. Moore's Tiffany School, the young man's imagination could not help but have been caught by Moore's unbounded admiration for the Islamic arts of North Africa and the Middle East. That Farnham turned to Orientalism in jewelry design was inevitable; moreover, nothing could have been more appropriate to show off the perfectionism of the jeweler's art than the intricate detailing, delicate ornament, and rich colorations of the Islamic world.

As a student, Farnham would have had at his disposal Tiffany's exemplary design library (assembled by Edward C. Moore). The collection included Owen Jones' two volumes of *Plans, Elevations, Sections, and Details of the Alhambra* with their large-scale chromolithographs of Islamic architectural detail, and a wealth of other works on Orientalism and Islamic Art such as: E. Collinot and A. de Beaumont's *Encyclopedia of Decorative Arts of the Orient*'s volumes on Arab and Persian ornament; Achille Prisse d'Avennes' *L'Art Arabe*; *Indian Domestic Architecture* by Louis Comfort Tiffany's friend and sometime partner Lockwood De Forest; and many lesser-known but richly illustrated works on Indian Jaipur enamels, the antiquities of Orissa, Turkish decoration, and Persian art.

Perhaps out of deference to Moore, Farnham would produce only one Orientalist jewel in his first important body of work: the cat's-eye pendant for the Paris Exposition of 1889. But after Moore's death in 1891, Farnham went on to produce significant collections of Orientalist designs for the World's Columbian Exposition of 1893 and the Paris Exposition of 1900. By this time, the style had become so popular that there were few fashionable American houses whose decor did not include a so-called Turkish Corner.

With the advent of the twentieth century, however, the taste for the richly ornamented and the exotic began to fade; and, in his designs for Buffalo's Pan-American Exposition of 1901, Farnham would abandon Orientalism entirely.

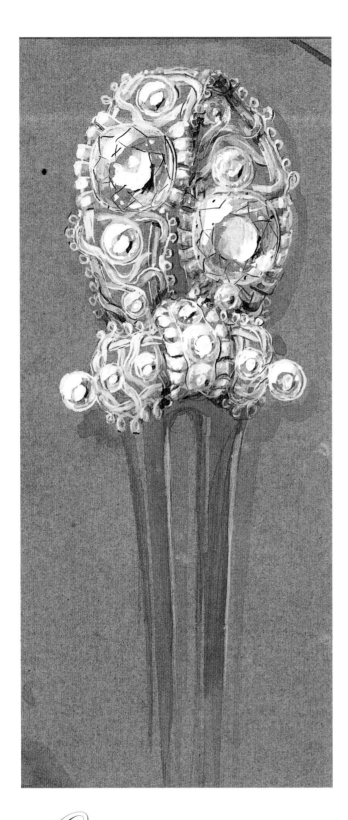

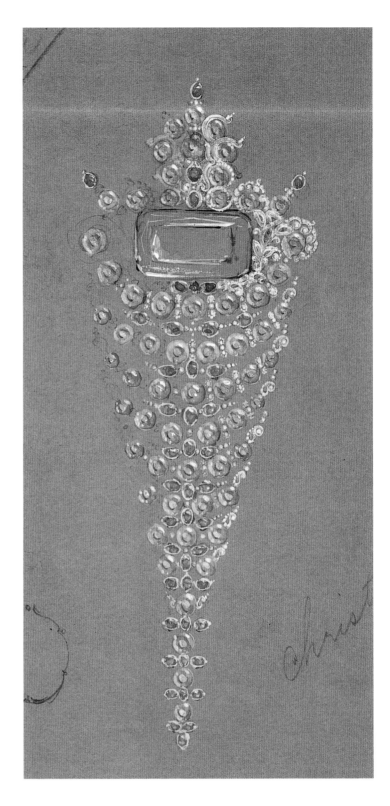

Orientalist jewelry began its rise to popularity following a display of Indian jewelry at London's Crystal Palace in 1851. It gained further prominence after 1876, when Parliament added "Empress of India" to Queen Victoria's many titles, and it remained in fashion until the early years of the twentieth century. This circa 1893 design for an Orientalist Art Nouveau hair ornament is set with two large diamonds and fourteen smaller rose-cut diamonds.

Drawing for the "Burmese" pendant brooch made for the 1893 Chicago Exposition. The French jewelry historian Henri Vever wrote in 1894, "An extremely flexible, large Burmese ornament, with beautifully warm and unusual color combinations obtained by using oriental rubies with Brazilian topaz. An aquamarine encrusted with pure gold and rubies is at its center." The price was $1,000.

Orientalist Brooch and drawing,
circa 1890–1900, set with a pink sapphire,
green garnets, yellow sapphires, diamonds,
and varicolored pearls.

Above:

The initial sketch for the "Arabesque" Arizona garnet necklace (originally an armlet) shown at the 1889 Paris Exposition.

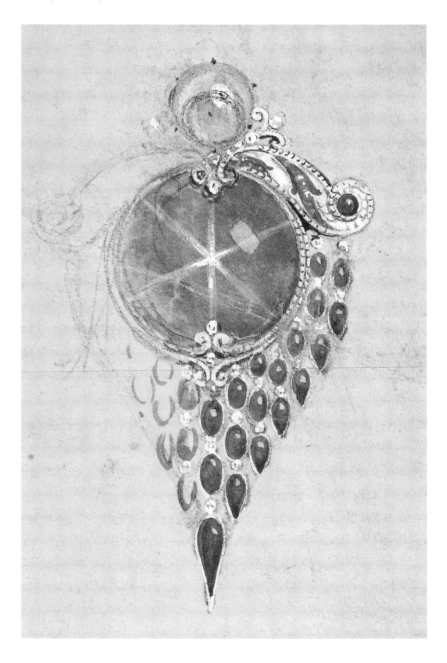

Right:

An alternative design for the "stomacher" (corsage ornament) featuring an exceptional ninety-carat star sapphire and thirty-nine small Burmese rubies shown at the Chicago Exposition; the final ornament, made from the same stones, had a green enamel snake encircling the star sapphire.

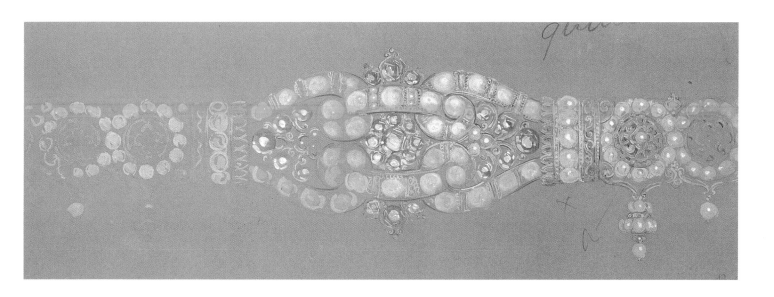

Circa 1893 designs for Orientalist jewelry.

Above:
Pearl-and-sapphire belt.

This necklace, centered by a large, scalloped-edge chrysoberyl, continues the Burmese style of the chrysoberyl-and-ruby bracelet shown at the World's Columbian Exposition in 1893.

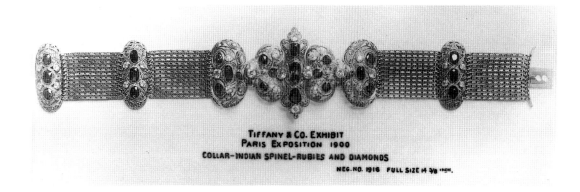

TIFFANY & CO. EXHIBIT
PARIS EXPOSITION 1900
COLLAR—INDIAN SPINEL—RUBIES AND DIAMONDS
NEG. NO. 1916 FULL SIZE 14 3/8 INCH.

Paulding Farnham's gold, Indian-style collar set with Indian spinels and diamonds was shown by Tiffany's at the 1900 Paris Exposition.

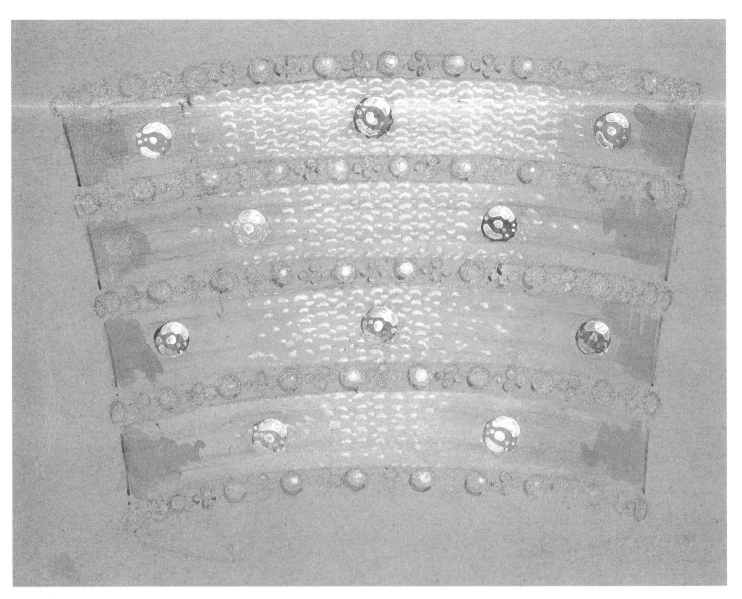

Above:
Design for Orientalist gold cuff bracelet
set with varicolored sapphires.

Right:
Circa 1893 drawing for an Orientalist
ring set with blue and pink sapphires.
Farnham used the curved, asymmetrical
Islamic *boteh* (pinecone) or "paisley"
shape in many of his ring designs,
of which this is one of the most
flamboyant.

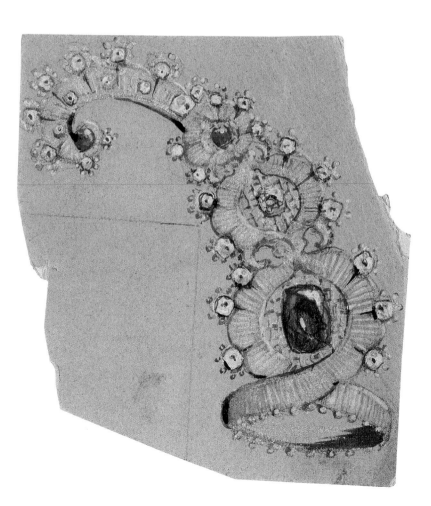

arnham based this circa 1893 "hand bracelet" on a traditional Indian wedding ornament called a *hathphul*. The top element circles the wrist, the central element covers the back of the hand, and the rings go over the fingers. It is studded with turquoises, sapphires, green garnets, zircons, peridots, hessionite garnets, beryls, tourmalines, chrysoberyls, and pearls.

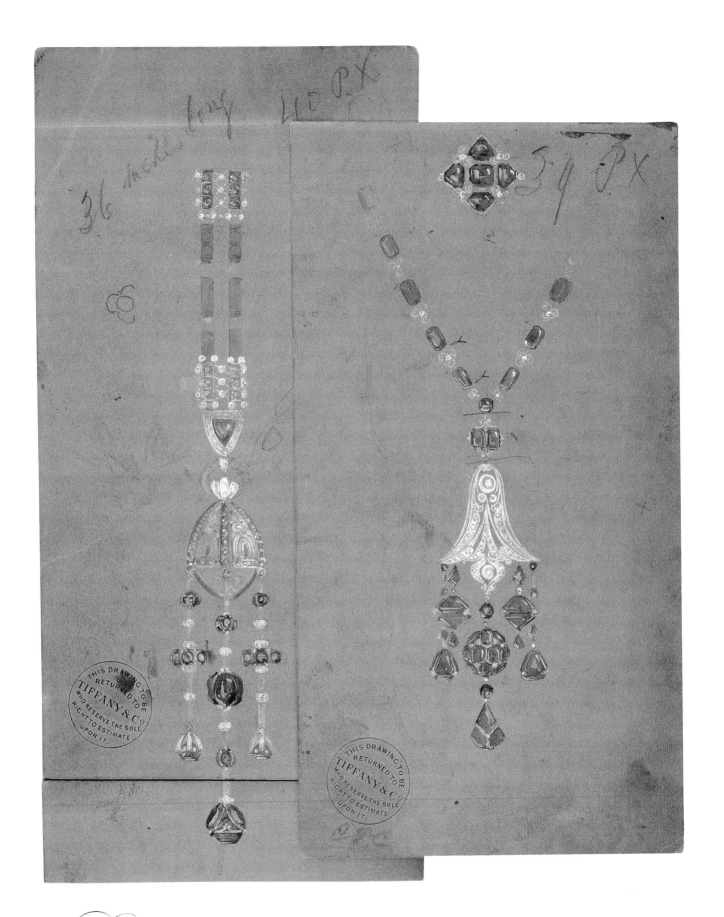

Drawings for two sautoir chains (long women's neck chains) shown at the 1900 Paris Exposition. Tiffany's catalogue described the chain on the left: "Demantoids and diamonds, large demantoids as pendant drops. Style, Russian." It sold for $5,500. The chain on the right was listed as "Double cut American sapphires with diamond pendant and odd shaped double sapphire and diamond drops." It sold for $3,000.

Opposite:
A similar pendant designed in the same Orientalist vein.

Orientalist brooch designs from the 1890s.

Above:
Brooch of pearls in a geometrical pattern.

Left:
Cabochon Mexican fire-opal brooch with four pearl accents. Tiffany gemologist George Frederick Kunz was particularly fond of the opals he purchased in Querétaro, Mexico, for Farnham's jewelry.

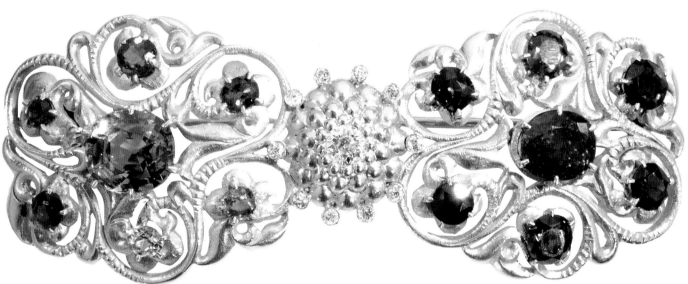

 op, left: drawing for two Indian-style multicolored jeweled buckles for the 1893 World's Columbian Exposition in Chicago. Bottom: a similar buckle designed to match the hand bracelet on page 83. Top, right: "Urchin Spray Aigrette" designed for the Chicago Exposition. The gold sea-urchin base was studded with antique Persian beads; the diamond-studded spun-glass aigrette was set in a large pear-shaped Peruvian emerald.

Right:

$\mathcal{T}$iffany's photograph of Farnham's black-pearl pendant shown at the 1889 Paris Exposition. *The Jewelers' Weekly* (June 20, 1889) reported, "The black pearl pendant is one of the most attractive jewels in the collection. It is formed of diamonds, mounted in a tasteful design, among them being set no less than eight large, black pearls, all from the Gulf of California. The pearls are elegantly matched, and the four larger ones, somewhat ovoid in form, are made into a pendant which hangs in a recess in the brooch, the largest pearl, in which the pendant terminates, being lower than the bottom of the brooch."

Above:

A preliminary drawing for the pendant.

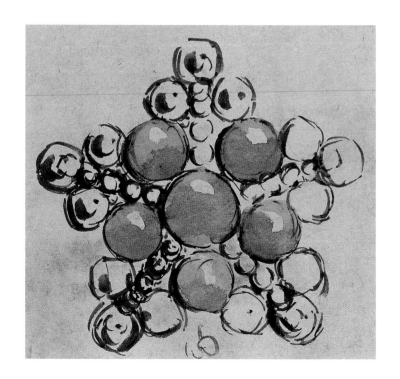

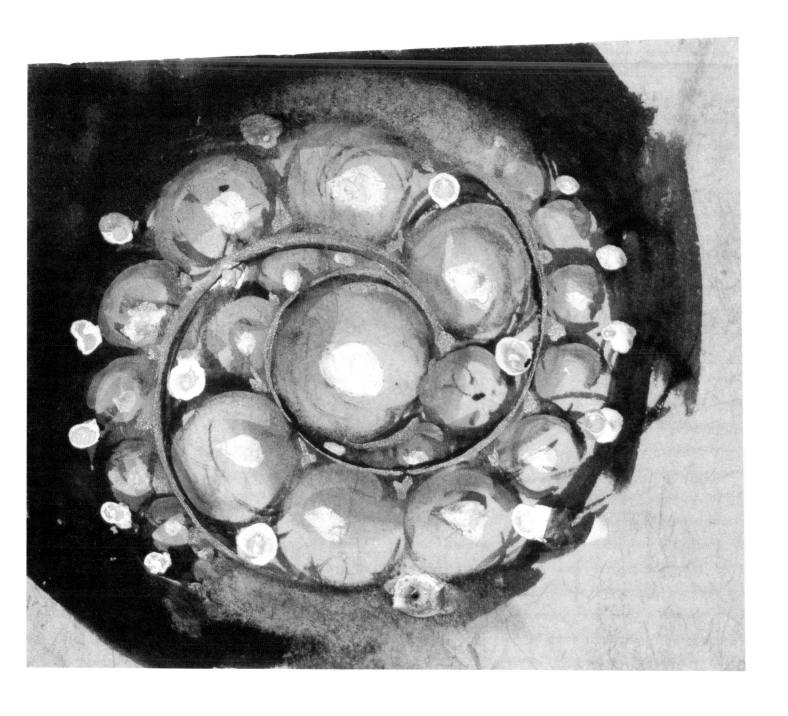

*C*irca 1889 design for a pearl, gold, and diamond spiral brooch. Spirally structured patterns are typical of both Islamic and Native American ceramic designs. This drawing has Farnham's characteristic freedom and vigor of line, and his equally characteristic, dramatic black shading.

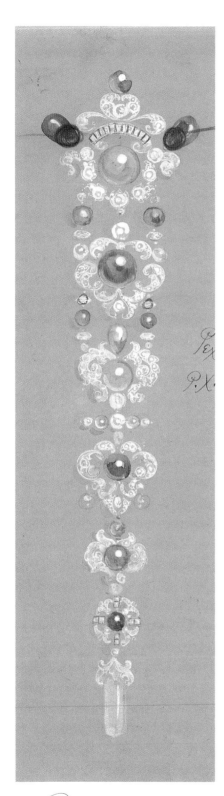

Original drawing and Tiffany's 1900 photo of a long pendant corsage ornament shown at the 1900 Paris Exposition. Made of platinum, it was set with varicolored Oriental pearls and diamonds.

The finished drawing and Tiffany's 1889 photo of a pentagonal cat's-eye pendant with diamond and ruby accents that was shown by Tiffany & Co. at the 1889 Paris Exposition. On June 13, 1889, *The Jewelers' Weekly* commented, "A necklace of Indian design is composed of a chain of fine gold wirework set with a diamond in the centre of each link. A beautiful pendant is suspended from it. This pendant is set with seven [sic] cat's eyes of remarkable size and beauty, with diamonds and rubies in gold wirework corresponding with that of the necklace. This necklace is distinctively Oriental, and is the most important article of its peculiar composition yet produced in this country. It is priced at $8,700."

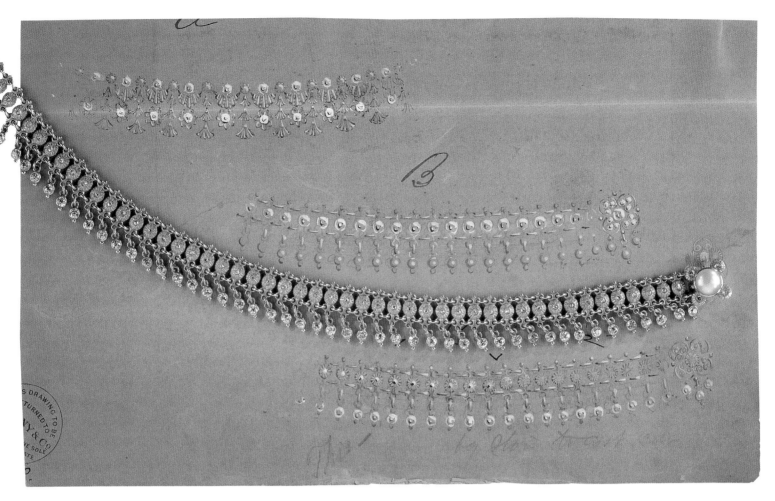

Above:

A light and intricate gold, enamel, and diamond
necklace designed by Farnham circa 1889,
placed upon his drawing of it and
similar necklaces.

Below:

Bonbonnière on a chain shown by Tiffany & Co.
at the 1889 Paris Exposition. The large
sapphires and painstaking workmanship suggest that
the piece was intended primarily for display.

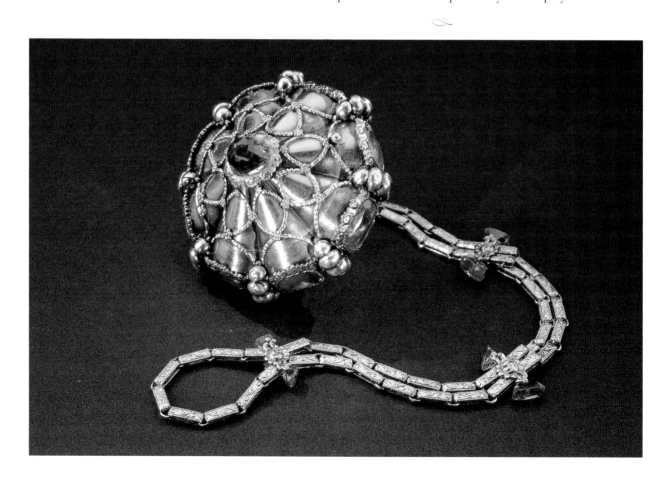

 rientalist eighteen-karat-gold and enamel "dog collar" studded with turquoises
and pearls, designed circa 1893.

*F*arnham embellished this carved
rock-crystal Moghul-style
inkwell with gold and enamel, studded
it with rubies, and placed a sapphire
on the finial of the cap.

Left:
*S*ilver-gilt and vivid pink enamel
coffee set studded with amethysts,
designed in 1902.

*M*oghul-style leather card case
with gold ornamentation studded with
Montana sapphires, designed for the 1893
Chicago Exposition. Note the caparisoned
elephants at the corners. Farnham's drawing
for the ornamentation is at left.

Opposite:

*N*ecklace of oval, round,
rectangular, square, and teardrop
amethysts in a geometric pattern held by
platinum chains studded with diamonds
and amethysts, designed circa 1901.

The Louis' REVIVAL

The Paris Exposition of 1889, where Paulding Farnham first gained international recognition, was France's bid for world leadership in modern design. With its great sky-scraping three-hundred-meter-high Eiffel Tower and other lesser feats of industrial engineering and architecture, it astonished the whole world, including America.

America's answer to Paris 1889, the Chicago World's Columbian Exposition of 1893, would take an entirely opposite artistic direction.

As Paris 1889 celebrated the one-hundredth anniversary of the French Revolution and the fall of the Bourbon monarchy under Louis XVI and Marie-Antoinette, it could hardly have made much of the late nineteenth century's popular Louis XIV, Louis XV, or Louis XVI Revival styles. However, Chicago 1893 embraced these styles with a vengeance.

Although the Louis' Revival, as it was loosely termed in America, covered the entire design vocabulary of eighteenth-century France, the focus was, for a number of reasons, clearly on the lighter, more neoclassical Louis XVI, from the later years of the eighteenth century. The Louis XVI mode, first of all, adapted best to the neoclassicism of America's own colonial George III and Federal styles; and, second, it was much favored by the Empress Eugénie of France, whom three generations of American women emulated and who in her own turn had positively hero-worshiped Louis XVI's queen, Marie-Antoinette.

By the time Paulding Farnham began work on his Tiffany jewelry collections for the Paris Exposition of 1889, the Louis' Revival of the 1880s was in full swing both in Europe and in America.

Young New York social leader Mrs. William K. Vanderbilt had spurred the revival with the main reception room of her new Richard Morris Hunt—designed mansion at Fifth Avenue and Fifty-second Street, decorated by the renowned Paris firm Jules Allard et Fils and inaugurated with a costume ball attended by all New York high society on March 26, 1883.

The room's airy Louis' Revival style, with its allegorical ceiling painting by Paris society artist Paul Baudry and Beauvais tapestry—hung walls, looked as much like a Belle Epoque Paris salon as possible and was a sharp contrast to the heaviness of the day's high Victorian eclecticism. It also contained the finest pieces of French furniture in America, a magnificent *secrétaire à abbatant* and matching *commode* made about 1787 by Jean-Henri Riesener for the apartment at the Château of Saint-Cloud belonging to none other than Marie-Antoinette.

Alva Vanderbilt followed up on this trend-setting French interior with America's greatest monument of the Louis' Revival style, Marble House, designed by Richard Morris Hunt and built on Bellevue Avenue in Newport, Rhode Island. It was completed on January 17, 1892, for Mrs. Vanderbilt's thirty-ninth birthday, the year before the World's Columbian Exposition, where the visually dominant Central Administration Building was also by Richard Morris Hunt, again in his neoclassical mode.

For the 1889 Paris fair, Farnham would design two major Louis XVI–style jewels, the "Colonial" yellow-diamond necklace and the "American Hazelnut" necklace, the latter named after the English essayist Thomas Carlyle's description of the principal diamonds of Marie Antoinette's legendary jewel as being "large as filberts" (hazelnuts). These were supported in the Tiffany display by a Louis XVI–style pearl-and-diamond collar, and another sapphire-and-diamond collar in the same style. For Chicago's World's Columbian Exposition, Farnham designed two monumental parures in modified but essentially Louis XVI style along with an important diamond corsage ornament of Louis XVI garlands; and of course he designed a dazzling emerald-and-diamond "Marie Antoinette" necklace based on a portrait of that unfortunate queen in London's Victoria & Albert Museum.

The taste for Louis' Revival design thrived in both Europe and America throughout the 1890s; and, for the Paris Exposition of 1900, Paulding Farnham would again design important Tiffany Louis XVI Revival jewels.

The style itself was for conservative American society both safe and in what was popularly considered good taste; however Paulding Farnham's frequently overscaled, highly colorful, and even at times flamboyant interpretations brought it an originality and dimension not seen in the works of its many other practitioners on both sides of the Atlantic.

he swags of this elaborate necklace of diamonds
set in platinum and gold were inspired
by late-eighteenth-century French jewelry.
Designed about 1900, it was made for
Ellen Garretson Wade, wife of Jeptha Homer
Wade II, a prominent Cleveland industrialist
who collected gemstones with the advice of
Tiffany's gemologist, George Frederick Kunz.
The necklace can be divided into a bracelet
and a shorter necklace, with or without
the central swags.

Right:
The necklace in its original Tiffany box.

Louis XVI Revival diamond necklace designed about 1900.

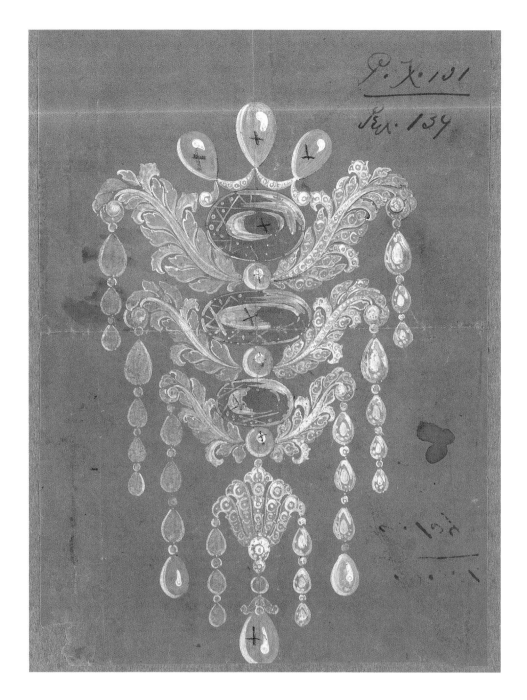

Opposite, top:

Brooch of Montana sapphires, freshwater pearls, and diamonds designed for the 1900 Paris Exposition.

Opposite, below:

Arizona garnet, pearl, and diamond brooch from the same period.

Tiffany's 1900 drawing and photograph for a pink topaz, pearl, and diamond brooch shown at the 1900 Paris Exposition. The largest topaz weighed 53.28 carats, and the pendant pearl weighed 93.25 grains. The brooch was priced at $17,500. This important jewel recalls the Louis XVI Revival pink-topaz parure that had been a highlight of Tiffany's display at the World's Columbian Exposition seven years earlier.

TIFFANY & CO. EXHIBIT
PARIS EXPOSITION 1900
BROOCH–PINK TOPAZ, PEARLS AND DIAMONDS

Two Louis XVI Revival pendant brooches designed in the 1890s.

Above:
Brooch with a tiara-style top, a central opal, and a pendant opal.

Opposite:
Brooch featuring an emerald flanked by pearls.

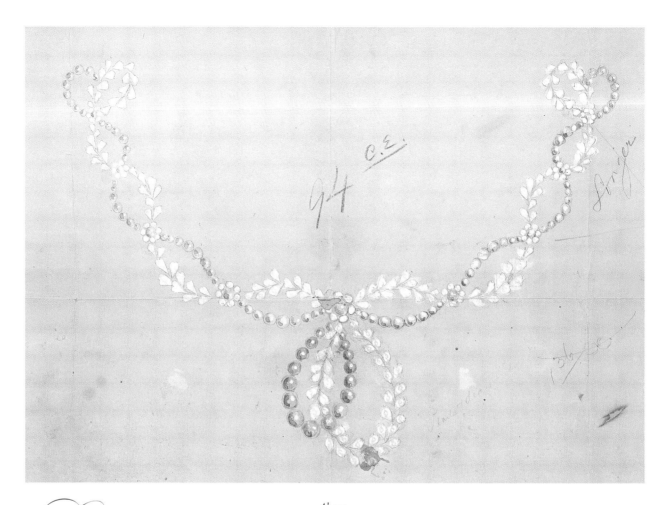

Drawing for a large diamond corsage ornament shown at the 1893 Chicago Exposition showing a strand of gray pearls that was not included in the finished piece. Tiffany's catalogue listed it as "108. Corsage Ornament. Representing a lattice of maidenhair fern, reaching from the center of the bust to either shoulder, each end forming into a loop, mounted in gold and set with 295 diamonds."

Drawing for the Portuguese-style necklace shown at the 1893 Chicago Exposition. Composed of 532 rose-cut diamonds, it was priced at $4,000.

rawing for a "giardinetto" (flower basket) brooch of diamonds, pearls, and two rubies for the World's Columbian Exposition. Although this design was apparently not executed, Tiffany's exhibit did include a "giardinetto" brooch of diamonds alone, plus five "giardinetto" rings in the Italian Renaissance style.

rawing for the emerald, pearl, and diamond bow necklace with pendant made by Tiffany's for the World's Columbian Exposition. Farnham based its design on the bow-knot necklace in Marie-Antoinette's portrait by François-Hubert Drouais at London's Victoria & Albert (then the South Kensington) Museum. The museum's director, A. B. Skinner, verified the accuracy of a tracing used to aid Farnham in his design. The largest emerald in the bow weighed sixty-six carats and the other four emeralds averaged over ten carats each; the necklace also contained four large pearls and 308 diamonds. Tiffany's sold the necklace for $12,000 on May 11, 1893, eleven days after the exposition opened.

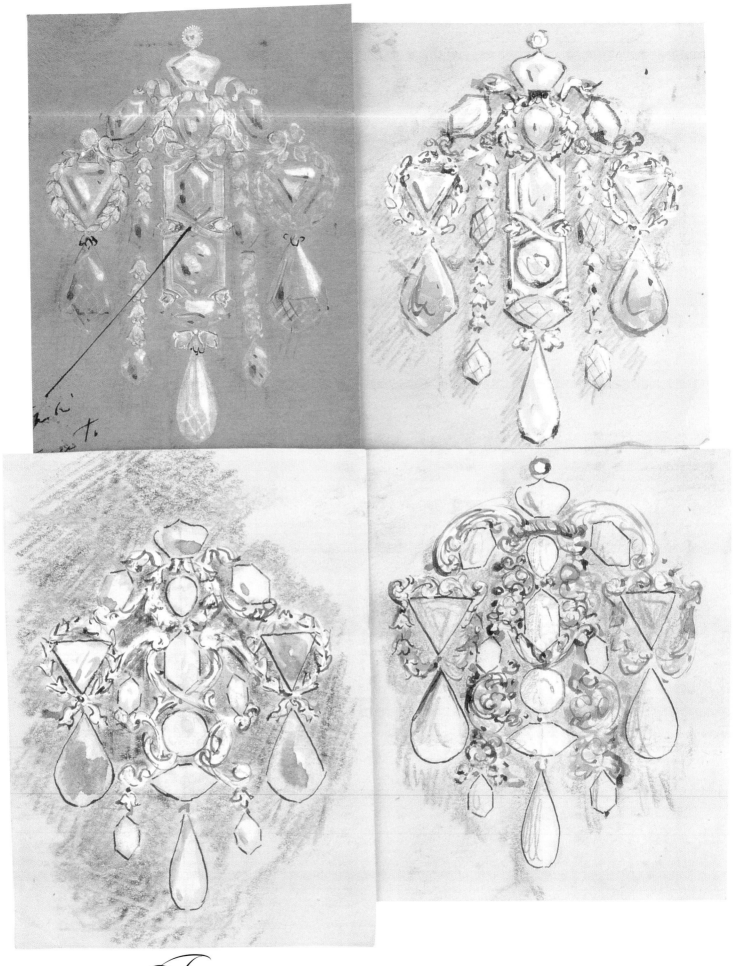

Farnham's studies for the Portuguese-style diamond pendant made by Tiffany's
for the World's Columbian Exposition.

The pendant contains yellow and
white diamonds, including
three unusual triangle-cut diamonds.
Priced at $2,900, it sold on April 17, 1893,
two weeks before the exposition opened.

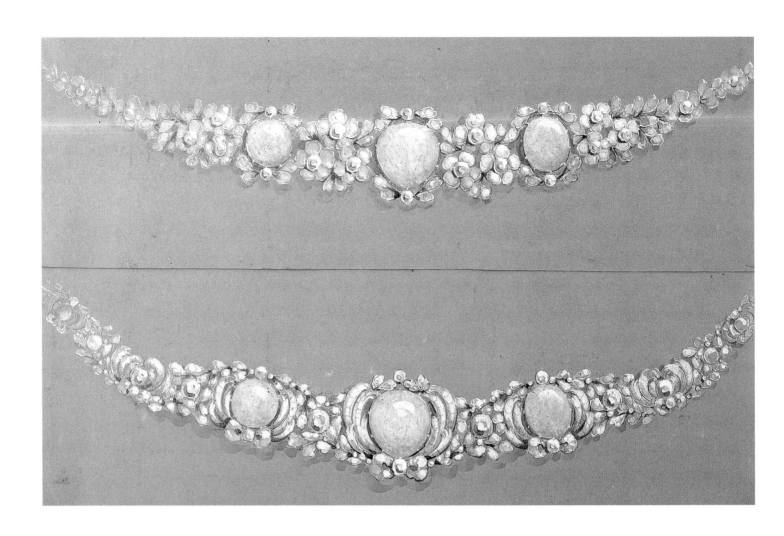

$\mathcal{T}$wo designs for a Hungarian-opal and diamond necklace.
In 1890 Tiffany gemologist George Frederick Kunz
traveled to Vienna to buy the last extraordinary Hungarian opals
shortly after the mines near Czernawitza—unable to compete
profitably with Australian production—were closed.
Farnham's designs were undoubtedly intended to
utilize three of these opals.

Opposite:
$\mathcal{S}$everal designs for the "Empire"-style
(actually Louis XVI Revival) diamond necklace
made by Tiffany's for the 1889 Paris
Exposition. The maidenhair fern motif
in the fourth design from the top was
adapted for the finished piece.

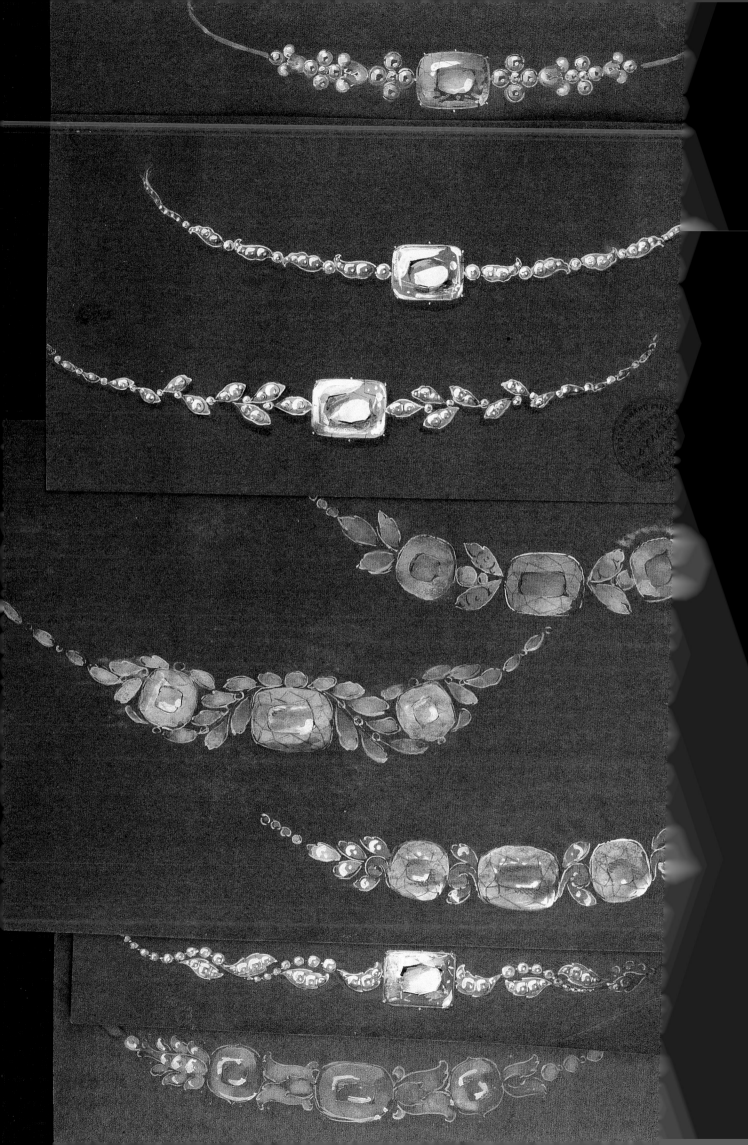

Alternate designs for the pearl-centered collar of a "lace" necklace made by Tiffany's for the 1889 Paris Exposition. On June 6, 1889, *The Jewelers' Weekly* described the finished piece, "A necklace of beautiful tracing of diamonds, representing a piece of lace, fastened in front by a cluster composed of a very large pearl, weighing 99 grains, surrounded by large diamonds, from which drops a delicate spray of diamond lace work…is a very handsome ornament…. It is valued at $8,000."

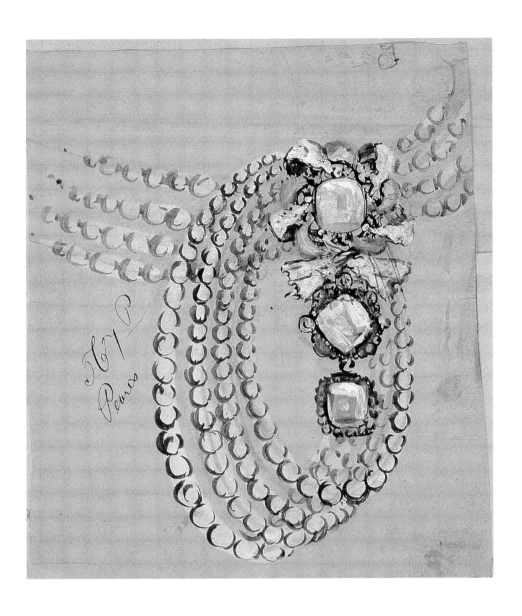

 Above:

*D*rawing for an Oriental pearl necklace
with a central emerald and diamond ornament;
the finished necklace was at the center of Tiffany's
main showcase at the 1889 Paris Exposition.

Right:
Tiffany's 1889 photograph shows the curved,
asymmetrical final arrangement of the
central ornament.

Circa 1889 watercolor sketch for an elaborately
jeweled buckle. The curving structure of the
jeweled motifs relate it to the emerald-and-
diamond center of Farnham's important Oriental
pearl necklace shown at the 1889 Paris Exposition;
both are in his "Hungarian" Louis XVI style.

Opposite:
A remarkably free circa 1890s
watercolor and pen-and-ink
sketch for a fleur-de-lis brooch.

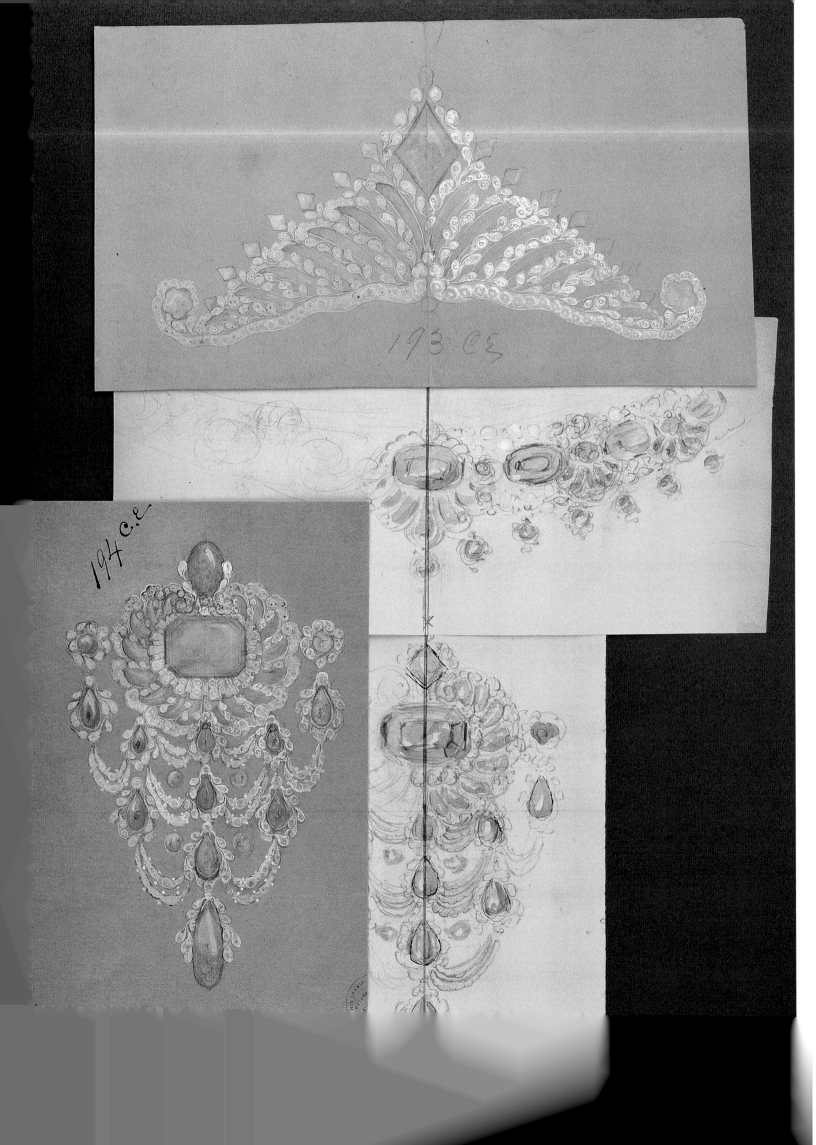

193 C.E

194 C.E

Designs for the parure set with "remarkable specimens of pink topaz" at the Chicago Exposition. The style of this parure—and the dominant style of Tiffany's jewelry exhibit in Chicago—was Louis XVI Revival, yet Tiffany's catalogue curiously described this parure's tiara as "Russian style" and its necklace as "Medieval." Background: preliminary drawings for the tiara and pendant brooch. Top: finished drawing for the tiara. Center: finished drawing for the pendant brooch, whose center was set with four large Russian pink topazes weighing a total of 71.75 carats; the briolette drop weighed 32.63 carats. The brooch was completed on April 3, 1893 and sold eight days later (before the exposition opened) for $4,000. Bottom: the necklace.

Opposite:

Designs for the elaborate aquamarine parure displayed at Chicago. It contained a total of 147 aquamarines—the largest weighing between 75 and 100 carats—all cut at Tiffany's gem-cutting shop from the same crystal to assure a uniform color. The parure also contained 1,848 diamonds. Background: preliminary drawings for the necklace and stomacher. Top: final drawing for the tiara. Bottom: final drawing for the stomacher. Set with seventy-two aquamarines and 803 diamonds, it was priced at $6,000.

Preliminary drawing for the tiara in the pink-topaz parure shown at the 1893 Chicago Exposition.

The imposing American turquoise and diamond tiara made for the 1900 Paris Exposition.

Above:
Drawing for the turquoise tiara.

Right:
A recent print from a 1900 glass negative
in the Tiffany & Co. Archives.

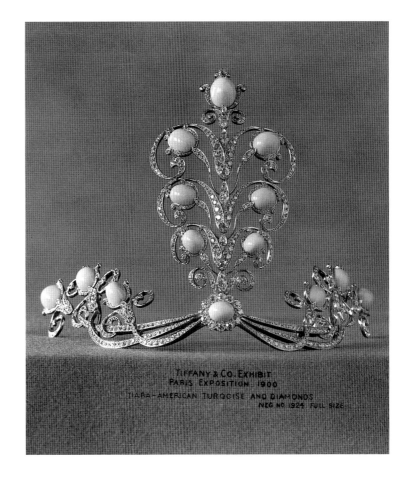

TIFFANY & CO. EXHIBIT
PARIS EXPOSITION 1900
TIARA—AMERICAN TURQOISE AND DIAMONDS
NEG NO 1924 FULL SIZE

Victorianism

ew possibilities of trade with far-off countries in the nineteenth century provoked cultural cross-pollination and an acquisitive urge. Fully evident at London's Great Exhibition of the Works of Industry of All Nations of 1851—and successfully reinforced by all the century's many succeeding world's fairs—the desire to collect the foreign, the fantastic, and even the peculiar was at the very heart of Victorianism.

Victorianism embraced not just one, but an entire United Nations of styles. It didn't pretend to be homogeneous. Its only common denominator was a fascination with craftsmanship of both man and machine, combined with a certain undercurrent of mixed sentimentality, latter-day Romanticism, and middle-class smugness that frequently caused it to overdo things.

At its best, it was democratic in its tastes and adventuresome in its exploration of the possibilities of newly discovered foreign styles.

In its 1878 edition, the *Gazette des Beaux-Arts* accurately summed up the situation as far as the jewelry industry was concerned: "It will be, without doubt, impossible at the present to create a new and individual style from all sorts of bits and pieces; but, it is permissible to try to rejuvenate the styles of other periods that were full of freshness and invention by appropriating them to our own uses, tastes and needs.

"Jewelers…we are off on an adventure, following only our personal fantasies, missing a school, having neither advice nor superior direction. We have only our clients' taste for luxury to support us."

As the three great powers of England, France, and the United States vied for both trade and territory, their ambitions played no small part in the Victorian panoramic vision of culture. Victorianism was, to a degree, the artful and artistic propaganda of Imperialism. Farnham's own sustained use of Native American themes was in step with the ideology of Manifest Destiny and its justification of the appropriation of the West by the United States.

All of Paulding Farnham's most productive years as a designer at Tiffany's were during the final years of the Victorian era (1885–1901), when the urge to eclecticism was fully mature. That his work was extremely eclectic itself was a result of those times and of the demands of Tiffany's public. Farnham excelled in the various Victorian modes of Orientalism, Naturalism, and the Louis XVI Revival style; and at the same time he ventured into revivalist styles of his own, such as Viking, Burmese, Russian, and Portuguese. In all of these, he showed considerable originality.

Neither Farnham himself nor Tiffany's catalogues of the period explain the choice of these four somewhat offbeat branches of Victorian revivalism; however, they are easily understandable in the context of Farnham's own artistic leanings, as well as those of Tiffany & Co. and its New York audience.

Farnham's simplification of Celtic interlace and its attenuated, abstract animals in his Viking style have clear affinities to his handling of the abstractions of Native American patternings. This Viking style furthermore acknowledged New York's very considerable Irish community.

Farnham's Burmese style falls, of course, under the broader heading of Orientalism, and at the same time it was appropriate to the American jewelry house that had the country's most important trade in Burma rubies and sapphires.

His so-called Russian style, although more Orientalist than truly Russian, may have been prompted by the love Tiffany's great gemologist George Frederick Kunz and Farnham shared for Russian gemstones, especially the green demantoid garnets from Russia's Ural mountains. Or perhaps it had simply been prompted by the elaborately patterned and colorful Russian enamels that Tiffany & Co. imported with such success from A. I. Kuzmichev in Moscow during the 1890s.

In the less-prominent Portuguese style, Farnham simply discovered a medium for using unusual and fascinating—if challenging— fancy-colored briolette diamonds to great advantage.

Hexagonal green-and-yellow-enamel pendant with pearls and diamonds,
made by Tiffany's for the 1889 Paris Exposition.

"Lotus Flower" brooch of pearls and diamonds set in gold, platinum, and pink-and-green enamel dating from the 1890s.

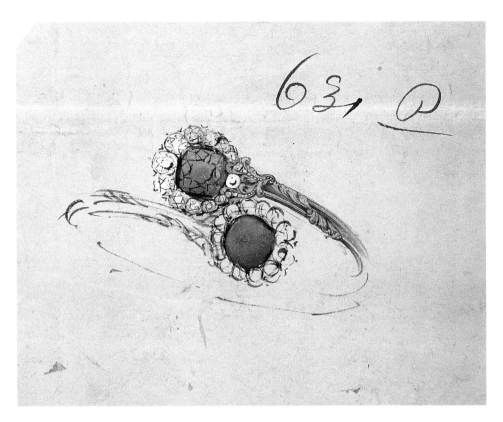

Drawing for the green tourmaline and red garnet "crossover" bracelet exhibited by Tiffany's at the 1889 Paris Exposition. The exceptionally fine garnet came from Arizona and the tourmaline from Maine. Both specimen American gemstones were provided by Tiffany gemologist George Frederick Kunz.

The "Cupid and Dove" châtelaine watch of carved moonstones with gold-and-diamond ribbons was made for the 1893 Chicago Exposition. In 1894, the French jewelry historian Henri Vever deemed it "more curious than beautiful." Tiffany's priced the watch at $1,200.

 his "bonnet brooch" with alternating bands of diamonds and green
garnets was shown at the 1893 Chicago Exposition. Tiffany's
catalogue listed it as "LOUIS XVIII. Bonnet-Brooch. Style of A.D. 1819."
It was priced at $600. The actual brooch is pictured on Farnham's
drawings for this and other bonnet brooches.

125

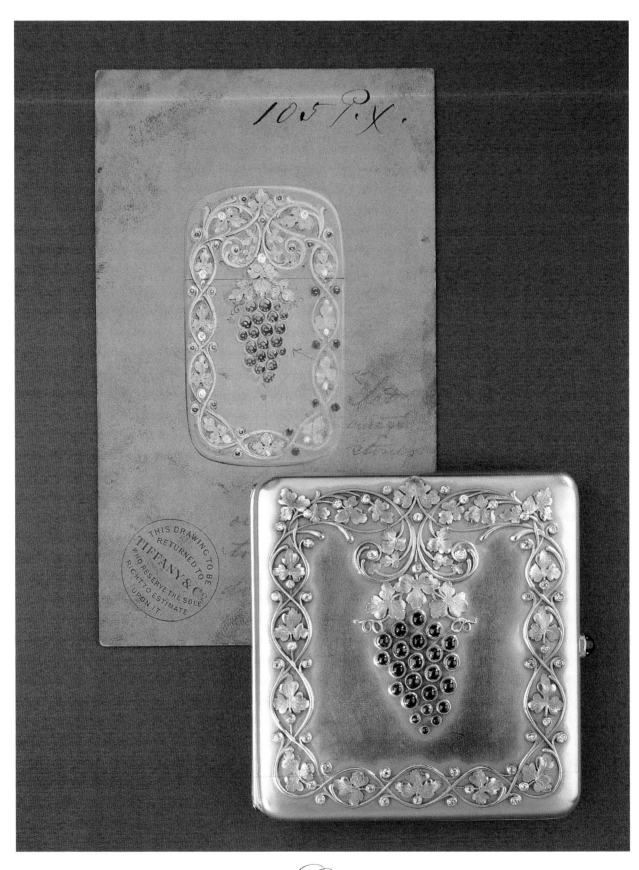

*G*old cigarette case with amethyst grapes,
diamond-studded grapevines, and a
sapphire-studded catch, designed for Tiffany's
display at the 1900 Exposition Universelle
in Paris; it was also shown the following year
at the Pan-American Exposition in Buffalo.
Above is Farnham's drawing of a match safe
of the same design.

*R*ock-crystal scent bottle with a gold neck; the hexagonal, diamond-rimmed stopper
is set with a cabochon amethyst. Designed circa 1899.

Right:

"*H*eart" rock-crystal vinaigrette
with a gold neck and stopper set with
diamonds and rubies; the platinum chain
and ring are studded with diamonds.
Designed in the 1890s.

*H*eavy gold bracelet studded with varicolored gemstones. The pure Art Nouveau style of this bracelet is unusual for Farnham. It corresponds with the amethyst, rock-crystal, and gold scent bottle in feeling—see page 127. Both were most likely designed around 1899, while the designer was working on mountings for Louis Comfort Tiffany's Favrile glass pieces shown at the 1900 Paris Exposition.

Opposite:
*P*aulding Farnham created the silver-gilt mounting set with pearls and aquamarines for Louis Comfort Tiffany's Favrile glass "Mermaid and Dolphin" vase, shown at the 1900 Paris Exposition. Louis Comfort Tiffany may have had reservations about allowing Farnham to mount his vases, but at least one critic admired them, writing in *The Art Interchange* that the vases were "rendered additionally attractive by gold mounting set with gems. The sapphires, turquoises, tourmalines and pearls join their varying colors to the opalescent hues of the glass and produce a never-ending play of color that the eye revels in."

Opposite:
Tiffany & Co.'s founder, Charles Lewis Tiffany, married Harriet Olivia Avery Young (sister of John Burnett Young, Tiffany's cofounder) on November 30, 1841. Farnham designed this gold Greek-revival cup with enamel decoration to commemorate their fiftieth (golden) wedding anniversary on November 30, 1891.

Foreground: a fifth century B.C. Athenian silver tetradrachma mounted in a gold brooch designed by Farnham. Background: designs for other settings of this coin.

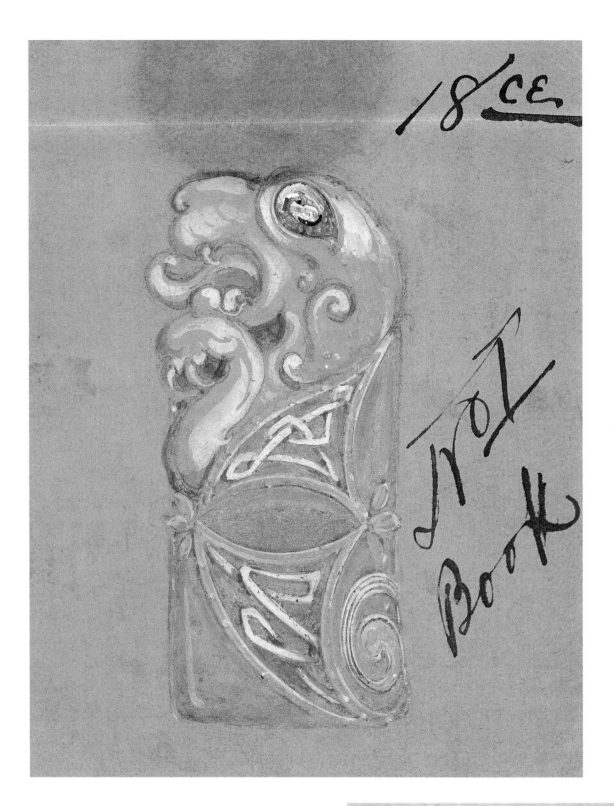

ketches for the Viking-style match
safe and ring shown at the 1893
Chicago Exposition.

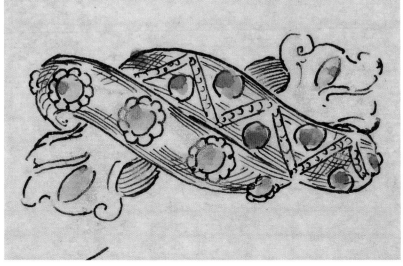

Above:

Bottles and powder-puff box decorated with enamel plaques and studded with semiprecious gems, from a silver-gilt Russian-style toilet set shown at the 1900 Exposition Universelle in Paris, the 1901 Pan-American Exposition in Buffalo, and the 1902 International Exposition of Modern Decorative Arts in Turin.

Right:

"Viking" sterling silver coffee service made by Tiffany & Co. for the 1901 Pan-American Exposition in Buffalo and also shown the following year at the International Exposition of Modern Decorative Arts in Turin. The service has interlacing Celtic-derived designs brightened with pale-green and lavender enamels and studded with zircons and hessonite garnets.

The Renaissance REVIEW

*I*n 1901, after sixty-four years on the English throne, Queen Victoria died and was succeeded by her eldest son, Edward VII.

The United States, too, would have a new leader in 1901. Following the assassination of President William McKinley at the Buffalo World's Fair, New Yorker Theodore Roosevelt became the twenty-sixth president of the United States.

The new century and the new Edwardian era brought with them marked cultural changes. The rather feminine romanticism, sentimentality, and elaborately detailed style of late Victorianism almost instantly disappeared and were replaced by a more pared-down, rugged, and masculine look in the first decade of the 1900s.

Although England's new king gave his name to the period, it could well have been called the Theodore Roosevelt era in the United States, so radical was the change brought to the government and to the personality of the times by the new president.

A revival of the late-Renaissance styles of such redoubtable men as Henry VIII of Tudor England, Francis I and his son Henry II of France, and the Holy Roman Emperor Charles V of most of the rest of Europe seemed appropriate as a style in the presidency of former Rough Rider Theodore Roosevelt. The Renaissance Revival style also provided early-twentieth-century Republican American capitalism with the authoritarian and somewhat daunting face it felt it required to reassure the public of its stability and, of course, its power.

Paulding Farnham excelled in this Revivalist style with his collections of Renaissance Revival jewelry for the Pan-American Exposition held in Buffalo in 1901, as well as in his designs for the Louisiana Purchase Exposition held in St. Louis three years later.

He was the acknowledged leader of the Renaissance Revival style in both American jewelry and silver. His gold-and-jeweled Adams Vase, begun in 1892 and completed in 1895 as a testimonial to Edward Dean Adams from the directors of his American Cotton Oil Company, is the most significant Neo-Renaissance object ever produced in America with its superbly crafted and opulent motifs of allegorical personages, plants, and animals. It was shown by Tiffany & Co. at the 1900 Paris Exposition, and the critical acclaim it received prompted Farnham to create a remarkable collection of Renaissance-style jewels composed of assorted nymphs and naiads mixed with more American flora and fauna for the Pan-American Exposition of 1901. All were rendered with the same exquisite Tiffany jewelry-shop craftsmanship of the Adams Vase, and, of course, all were encrusted with American pearls and gemstones.

For St. Louis, Farnham created a massive Neo-Renaissance gold, enamel, and diamond necklace (of proportions more suitable to the coronation regalia of a European monarch than to the evening dress of an American socialite). His most publicized design for St. Louis 1904 was, however, an extensive and massive silver tea set and table service in high Renaissance style, lavishly ornamented with sphinxes, caryatids, floral garlands, and scrolls. There was also a gold dressing table set of infinitely elaborate Florentine design once again combining the style's requisite nymphs, naiads, and caryatids all tied together with the requisite scrolls and garlands of flowers, and all presided over by the muses of comedy and tragedy, Thalia and Melpomene, atop the set's cologne bottles.

Farnham's works for both world's fairs, with their fantastic combinations of the era's recently acquired vocabulary of late-fifteenth- and early-sixteenth-century Renaissance and Mannerist ornament, drew together all the extraordinary talents of Tiffany & Co.'s goldsmiths, silversmiths, gemologists, sculptors, and enamelers, and showed them off to the great advantage of Tiffany's.

*old-and-enamel Renaissance Revival brooch
set with varicolored sapphires and diamonds
designed for the 1900 Paris Exposition.*

Circa 1893 Renaissance Revival jewels designed by Paulding Farnham featuring varicolored sapphires promoted by Tiffany gemologist George Frederick Kunz. When Kunz showed some colored gems to Oscar Wilde, he responded enthusiastically, "I see a renaissance of art, a new vogue in jewelry in this idea of yours. Bah! who cares for the conservatives! Give them their costly jewels and conventional settings. Let me have these broken lights—these harmonies and dissonances of color."

Top:
A gold-and-enamel bracelet set with varicolored sapphires and diamonds.

Above, right:
This gold-and-platinum "giardinetto" ring with rubies, diamonds, and varicolored sapphires was exhibited at the 1893 Chicago Exposition.

Above, left:
Gold ring with rubies, diamonds, and varicolored sapphires.

Farnham's diamond setting for a 162.5-carat sapphire shown at the 1893 Chicago Exposition. The brooch was priced at a princely $27,000.

TIFFANY & CO. EXHIBIT
PARIS EXPOSITION 1900
BROOCH, 7 LARGE PEARLS ETC.
NEG. NO. 1905. FULL SIZE

This brooch of strikingly unusual coloration—seven large black pearls and numerous yellow and white diamonds—was designed for the 1900 Paris Exposition.

Left:
Tiffany's 1900 photograph.

Opposite:
Farnham's drawing.

Design for a Renaissance Revival corsage
ornament featuring large baroque pearls,
intended for the 1901 Buffalo
Exposition.

*G*old pendant with two chased female figures
set with emeralds, rubies, diamonds, and
large American pearls. This was one of many
similar Italian Renaissance–style jewels that
Farnham designed for Buffalo.

 circa 1901–04 drawing for a Renaissance Revival
pendant with a large star ruby.

Right:

 heart-shaped opal pendant designed about 1901,
placed upon a sketch of a similar pendant.

DWTS.

MAKING.

SELL STORE.

92566

DWTS.

MAKING.

*P*aulding Farnham's "Holbein Pendant," shown by Tiffany's
at the 1901 Buffalo Exposition. It was based on a design
in the British Museum by Hans Holbein the Younger
(1497?–1543), the painter famous for his brilliant
portraits of Henry VII and his court.

Opposite:
*R*enaissance Revival demi-parure comprising
a bracelet, a necklace, a brooch, and a pair of earrings
designed about 1901–04.

Farnham designed this Renaissance Revival silver casserole in 1905.
The decorative motifs and strapwork on the body and lid are
characteristic of Renaissance silver, and the winged figure on
the handle is taken from Renaissance sculpture.
The lid has a rabbit finial.

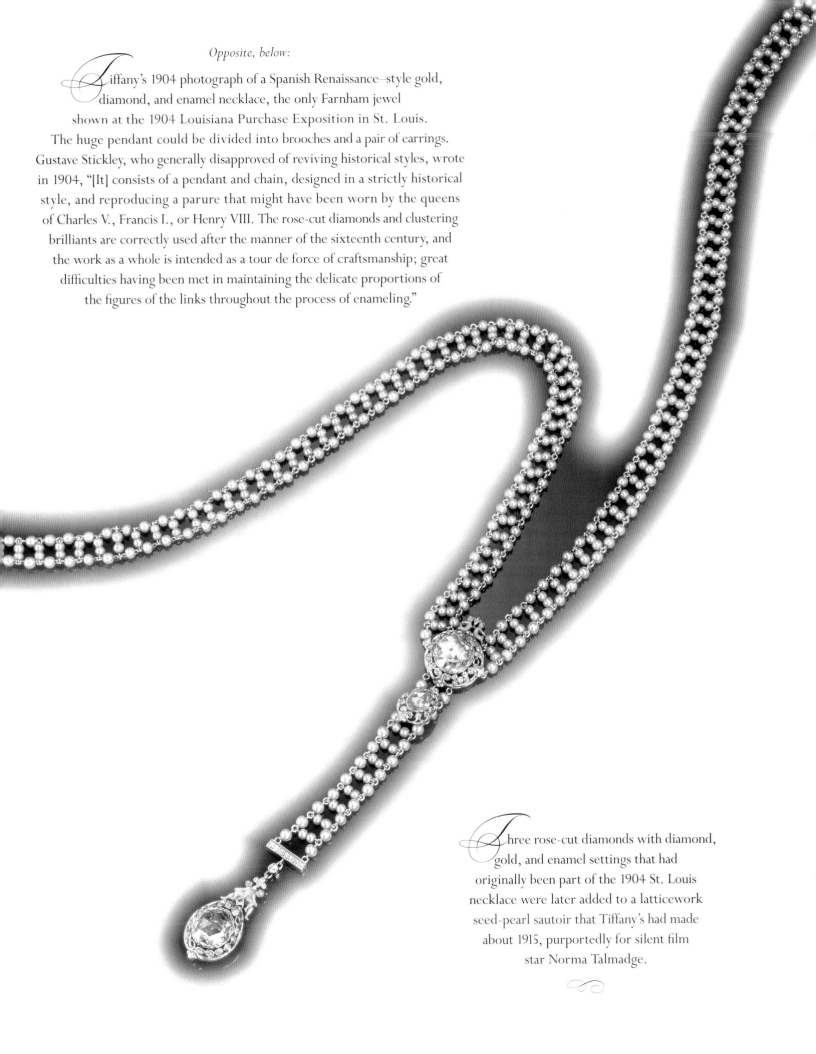

Opposite, below:

Tiffany's 1904 photograph of a Spanish Renaissance–style gold, diamond, and enamel necklace, the only Farnham jewel shown at the 1904 Louisiana Purchase Exposition in St. Louis. The huge pendant could be divided into brooches and a pair of earrings. Gustave Stickley, who generally disapproved of reviving historical styles, wrote in 1904, "[It] consists of a pendant and chain, designed in a strictly historical style, and reproducing a parure that might have been worn by the queens of Charles V., Francis I., or Henry VIII. The rose-cut diamonds and clustering brilliants are correctly used after the manner of the sixteenth century, and the work as a whole is intended as a tour de force of craftsmanship; great difficulties having been met in maintaining the delicate proportions of the figures of the links throughout the process of enameling."

Three rose-cut diamonds with diamond, gold, and enamel settings that had originally been part of the 1904 St. Louis necklace were later added to a latticework seed-pearl sautoir that Tiffany's had made about 1915, purportedly for silent film star Norma Talmadge.

1859

George Paulding Farnham (usually called Paulding or Paul) is born on November 6 to George and Julia Paulding Farnham, who were living in the Farnham family house at 171 Sullivan Street, New York City. (The Paulding family house still stands nearby at 24 Charlton Street.)

1866

Moves with his parents and Farnham uncles, aunts, and grandparents to Elizabeth, New Jersey.

1868

Moves with his parents to a house they purchase at 114 Rahway Avenue in Elizabeth.

c.1879

Under the aegis of his uncle, Tiffany & Co. Vice President Charles T. Cook, Farnham becomes a student-apprentice at Tiffany's, working primarily with chief designer Edward C. Moore.

1882

June 3: Farnham's earliest dated Tiffany jewelry design, for an Orientalist jeweled belt.

1885

November 1: Tiffany's hires Farnham as Moore's general assistant for $55 per week.

November 6 (Farnham's twenty-sixth birthday): *New York Town Topics* praises an enameled chrysanthemum brooch that he designed.

1886

November 1: Tiffany's raises his salary to $65 per week.

1887

Begins work on jewelry designs for the 1889 Exposition Universelle in Paris.

November 1: Tiffany's raises his salary to $77 per week.

1888

June 5: Tiffany's board elects him a member.

November 1: Tiffany's raises his salary to $87 per week.

1889

March: Tiffany's displays the jewelry he designed for the Paris Exposition at its New York store.

May 6: Attends the opening of the Paris Exposition. Wins wide acclaim for his enamel and jeweled floral jewelry, particularly for an extraordinary series of twenty-four orchid brooches, each depicting a different variety. His jewels based on Native American designs garner equally high praise. Tiffany's awarded gold medal for Farnham's jewelry.

October 22: Usher at the wedding of Edward C. Moore's youngest son, John Chandler Moore, and Corinne de Bebian.

November 1: Tiffany's raises his salary to $96 per week.

1890

Resides at 142 East Eighteenth Street in New York.

April: In New York, Tiffany's displays new versions of the orchid brooches shown in Paris, plus a series of newly designed orchid brooches depicting additional varieties, thirty-nine in all.

1891

Begins designs for Tiffany & Co.'s display at the 1893 World's Columbian Exposition in Chicago.

Tiffany's board appoints him assistant secretary. After Edward C. Moore's death on August 2, the board appoints him secretary and transfer clerk; he becomes the head of the jewelry department, and John T. Curran becomes chief silver designer.

Moves to the Union League Club at 431 Fifth Avenue.

November 30: An eighteen-carat gold cup that Farnham designed is presented to Charles L. Tiffany, founder and president of the company, on the occasion of his and his wife's fiftieth wedding anniversary.

1892

Begins work on the Adams Vase, a commemorative gold cup studded with semiprecious stones and pearls.

September 1: Tiffany's raises his salary to $135 per week.

October: New York City's Committee of One Hundred awards him the first-prize gold medal for his decorations on Tiffany's Union Square store celebrating the four-hundredth anniversary of Columbus's discovery of America.

1893

May 1: Chicago World's Columbian Exposition opens. His most important jewels are in the Louis XVI Revival style, including important aquamarine and pink-topaz parures. He also displays a broad array of Orientalist jewelry, floral jewels, jewels depicting small animals and insects, and inlaid silver vases based on Pueblo pottery.

1894

Sculpts a bronze bust of Charles L. Tiffany.

1895

May: Exhibits a plaster sculpture titled *Phoenecia and the Wind* at the National Sculpture Society's show in the Fine Arts Building, 215 West Fifty-seventh Street, New York; it was priced at $2,000. The nude female figure symbolized the Phoenician nation, thought to have invented sailpower for ships. Farnham, a sailing enthusiast, later joined the New York Yacht Club.

November 6: Directors of the American Cotton Oil Co. present the Farnham-designed Adams Vase to their chairman, Edward Dean Adams.

1896

June 2: August Belmont II wins the magnificent Farnham-designed Belmont Stakes trophy that he had commissioned. Farnham continues to design trophies awarded to Belmont Stakes winners through 1907.

June 25: Farnham is injured in a cable-car accident widely reported in the New York press.

August 12: Farnham's father dies of heat prostration just before his sixty-fourth birthday; a heat wave reaching 103° killed 177 New Yorkers on that day alone.

August 29: Proposes marriage to Sarah ("Sally") Welles James, daughter of Colonel Edward C. James, a prominent New York lawyer.

December 31: Marries Sally at St. John's (Episcopal) Church in her hometown, Ogdensburg, New York. *The New York Times* reports the following day, "The bride wore a white satin dress trimmed with point duchesse lace, low neck and short sleeves, and wore a diamond and ruby crescent, the gift of the groom." He is thirty-seven years old; she is twenty-seven.

1897

January: The newlyweds honeymoon in Montreal and then move to 21 West Thirty-first Street in New York.

May 26: His mother dies at the age of sixty. Inherits her country house in Great Neck on Long Island's north shore and moves there with Sally.

Begins designing jewelry and silver for the 1900 Paris Exposition.

1898

January 10: Son James ("Jim") Paulding Farnham born in Great Neck.

Designs the gold sword presented to Admiral George Dewey in recognition of his victory at Manila Bay. (The sword is now in the United States Naval Academy Museum.)

1899

John T. Curran leaves Tiffany & Co.; Farnham takes over his position as chief silver designer.

1900

April 14: Paris Exposition opens. His most successful jewels are a spectacular iris brooch of Montana sapphires and green garnets, the "Wild Rose Branch" of pink tourmalines and emeralds, the "Aztec" necklace of Mexican fire opals and red tourmalines, and a tiara set with American turquoises. The Adams Vase and silver vases based on Native American designs win wide acclaim. Farnham's other works include jeweled mounts for Louis Comfort Tiffany's Favrile glass vases and perfume flasks. He wins two gold medals and Tiffany & Co. wins the grand prize for jewelry.

November 27: Daughter Julia Paulding Farnham born.

1901

March 24: Sally Farnham is with her father when he dies in Palm Beach, Florida.

May 1: Pan-American Exposition in Buffalo, New York, opens. Tiffany's display includes Farnham's pink tourmaline "Lawson Pink" carnation brooch, a Montana-sapphire and diamond "Bird-of-Paradise" corsage ornament, a broad array of Renaissance Revival jewels, and a series of abstract floral jewels. His most important work in silver is the "Viking"-style coffee service.

Sally begins her career as a sculptor under the tutelage of her husband and her friend Frederic Remington, the sculptor and painter of the American West who also hailed from Ogdensburg, New York.

1902

February 18: Charles L. Tiffany dies at the age of ninety; Charles T. Cook, third largest shareholder in Tiffany & Co., becomes president. Louis Comfort Tiffany inherits a major share of his father's estate and takes over as the company's design director.

1904

April 30: Louisiana Purchase Exposition in St. Louis opens. Tiffany & Co.'s display includes only one Farnham jewel, a massive Renaissance Revival necklace; Louis Comfort Tiffany's much more extensive jewelry display wins broad critical acclaim. The company's exhibit also includes Farnham's Renaissance Revival silver tea and coffee service and lesser objects. His sculptures shown include *Psyche*, the White Rock sparkling water trademark, and the dog Nipper for the Victor Talking Machine Co.'s life-size version of its world-famous "His Master's Voice" trademark.

1905
August 31: Tiffany & Co. completes Farnham's magnificent silver, copper, and jeweled "Aztec" bowl.

1907
January 26: Charles T. Cook dies at the age of seventy-one. John Chandler Moore succeeds him as president, and Louis Comfort Tiffany takes over as Tiffany & Co.'s chief jewelry designer.

July 5: Son John Paulding Farnham born.

1908
June 2: Resigns from Tiffany & Co.

Until 1912, works as a sculptor at a studio at 57 West Fifty-seventh Street, New York.

1912
June 21: Leaves New York for what turned out to be extended travels in the western United States and Canada, at some point moving to California. Invests in various unsuccessful gold-mining operations.

1914
July 27: Sally Farnham files a petition for divorce in Milford, Pennsylvania, on the grounds of her husband's desertion.

1915
August 2: Sally's divorce petition is granted.

1920
Farnham is in Oakland, California, boarding in the house of Ida Edson Solomon, at 3611 Dimond Avenue; she is a fifty-five-year-old widow with four grown children.

January: Exhibits paintings from his historical marine series titled "Ancient Ships of the Merchant Marine that Opened the Commerce of the World" at the Hotel Oakland.

1921
Has a studio at 1441 Broadway in Oakland.

April 19: President Warren G. Harding unveils Sally Farnham's best-known work, the equestrian statue of Simón Bolívar now standing at the Avenue of the Americas entrance to New York's Central Park.

1923
Now living in Mill Valley, California; travels to New York and Washington to arrange exhibitions of his historical marine series.

1924
April–May: Travels to accompany exhibitions of twelve paintings from his historical marine series at the Corcoran Gallery of Art in Washington, D.C., April 1–22; the Baltimore Museum of Art, April 24–May 5; and the Robert C. Vose Gallery in Boston, May 10–24.

August 2: Makes a will leaving "all my worldly goods…to my friend Mrs. Ida Edson Solomon" shortly before undergoing surgery at the Providence Hospital in Oakland.

1926
December: Visits New York City, staying at the Prince George Hotel.

1927
August 10: Dies at the age of sixty-eight at Agnew State Hospital in Santa Clara County, California. His death certificate and accounts of his death list his widow as Ida Farnham.

August 13: Service held in a funeral chapel at 1123 Sutter Street, San Francisco.

1930
April 3–5: The estate of Max Williams, an art dealer and collector, auctions Farnham's nineteen historical marine paintings for $2,300 at the Haaseman Gallery in New York.

1943
April 28: Sally Farnham dies at the age of seventy-three in New York.

August–October: Farnham's historical marine series is exhibited at the Savoy Art and Auction Galleries in New York prior to its October auction.

October 7–8: Paulding Farnham's historical marine series and Sally Farnham's personal property and sculptures are auctioned at the Savoy Galleries. (The marine series is now at the Art Gallery of the University of Pittsburgh.)